CONTENTS

PREFACE

Paddy Cole and Tim Ryan have been friends for a few years now since they were first introduced by publican Dessie Hynes. They discussed the idea of a biography, and Tim recorded a series of interviews with Paddy in the summer of '95.

A graduate of English and Latin from University College, Cork, Tim Ryan is a former political reporter with the *Irish Press*. He is the author of three previous biographies — *Mara* (1992), *Dick Spring: A Safe Pair of Hands* (1993) and *Albert Reynolds: The Longford Leader* (1994).

"The man that hath no music in himself,
Nor is not moved by concord of sweet sounds,
Is fit for treasons, strategems and spoils;
The motions of his spirit are dull as night,
And his affections dark as Erebus:
Let no such man be trusted. Mark the music."

(Shakespeare: The Merchant of Venice)

Paddy Cole and Tim Ryan

1

KING OF THE SAX — AT 12!

Main Street, Castleblaney, 1951. People are crowding into the Lyric Theatre for a concert featuring the very popular Maurice Lynch Band, a local outfit. On the door outside a poster proudly announces: 'The Maurice Lynch Band, featuring Ireland's youngest saxophone player, 12-year-old Paddy Cole!'

The band arrives on stage. Young Paddy Cole, shaking with fear, clutches his instrument as the music starts. The youngster is terror-stricken, freezes and misses the melody.

The problem is saved by an alert Paddy Cole Snr, who is playing beside his son, and quickly takes his role. Eventually Junior gets his nerve and starts up. His Dad returns to his stand and the tune continues. It was an inauspicious start to the career of one of Ireland's best known musicians.

Paddy Cole Snr had pioneered the playing of the saxophone in the strongly musical town of Castleblaney, Co. Monaghan.

'He, like others, was a real pioneer in his field because he had nobody to teach him how to play, and nobody to listen to,' says his son. 'He and his pals would play an old 78 record in the kitchen and pick out the music themselves. It was real dedication.'

The Cole family had music in their blood. A cousin, Francy Cole, had written some modern pieces of jazz and was far ahead of his time, but like many artists, did not receive any real appreciation in his own lifetime. The family even had their own 'Cole's Number 1 Band', which consisted of Harry, Francy and Paddy Snr.

Paddy Cole Jnr was born on Castleblaney's Henry St. on 17 December, 1939. The site is now occupied by a shoe store. Shortly after his birth the family moved to Lakeview on the Armagh Road, where his mother and older sister still live.

Paddy Cole was the only son, and second eldest, in a family of seven. His sisters, Sadie, Mae, Carmel, Jacinta, Lucia and Betty inherited the family's musical talent. Lucia studied music in Cambridge. Jacinta played in a group with Stevie Sewell and Patrice McNeill, who ended up a singer in her own right.

The group was playing in the Three Star Inn in Castleblaney on the night it was bombed on 7 March, 1976. The place collapsed around them and one man, Pat Mohan was killed when he touched a car outside, triggering the bomb. The town was devastated. Paddy Cole was on his way back from Canada with the Superstars when he heard the news.

'We few into Kennedy Airport in New York from Canada where we had being playing and we picked up the papers on the Aer Lingus flight to Dublin. We were dumbstruck when we read the headlines about the bombing. There were no details of the deaths or injuries, but wee Jimmy Smyth, a brother of Patrice, and myself knew the group played there every Sunday night. We were in a dreadful state until we got home. Luckily they were all right.'

Jacinta Cole still plays music and is actively involved in amateur drama in Monaghan.

Carmel Cole, who describes herself as "the clapper in the family; I clapped for the rest of them" — did not play an instrument, but her husband, Ronnie Duffy is the drummer with Big Tom and the Mainliners. Their young son, Mark, is now the drummer in Cathy Durcan's band. Another of Paddy's sisters, Lucia, who has worked on RTE's early morning TV programme, was voted television and radio personality of the year in Qatar, where she lived for many years. Mae, unusually for a young girl, also learned to play the saxophone.

The family's terraced home on the Armagh Road is just a few miles from the Border. Across the road was a Customs Post, since closed. One of Paddy's earliest memories is of pigs squealing in morning outside the family home.

'The customs officers used to seize lorry loads of pigs which were being smuggled across the border during the night, and they would park the lorries for checking outside the Customs Post before sending them on elsewhere. I can still remember the loud squealing that would wake you up in the early morning,' he recalls.

'The big smugglers were like heroes or gangster characters to us young fellows. These guys used to lead the customs boys a merry dance in the hills along the border.'

One day the officers arrived into a pub in the town to arrest a man suspected of smuggling butter. The man hit a secret switch in his car and it exploded in flames outside. The butter caught fire too, and flowed down the street. There was pandemonium.

Most families in 'Blaney engaged in a little 'small-time smuggling' to obtain goods not available south of the border. Paraffin oil and white bread were keenly sought after. Young Paddy Cole and his mates would take the train to Culloville and then walk up to Crossmaglen. There they bought a few gallons of paraffin oil and six loaves of white bread each.

'On the way back down the road to Culloville if we met a customs patrol we immediately threw the bread and paraffin over the hedge and walked on for a few hundred yards until it was safe to go back and collect it. I remember once bringing oil from Crossmaglen down the two or three miles to Culloville only to discover a pin-hole in the bottom of the bloody can! And there I was trying to keep my finger over the bottom of the can the whole way down, and on the train afterwards!' Life was not easy for a young amateur smuggler!

Smuggling was a way of life for many, an addiction for some. There was little trouble on the border in the '40s and early '50s as Paddy Cole grew up. But politics was a sensitive subject, particularly at election time. Then friend fought friend, neighbour fell out with neighbour.

'My mother and father were Fianna Fáil supporters, but not active. De Valera was huge in our house.'

The memory of visits by James Mathew Dillon, or 'James Mathew' as he was known locally, to Castleblaney are clearly etched in Paddy Cole's memory.

'There would be torchlight parades when James Mathew came to town, but the Fianna Fáilers used to come out on the street in force. There would be fisticuffs galore.'

Dillon used to address the crowds from the window of Malone's pub, later owned by Paddy Cole, and now 'The Gunner Brady's' on Main St. Paddy Cole Snr was once shocked to hear that someone had seen Fianna Fáil and Fine Gael TDs having their lunch together in Dáil Eireann. He could not believe that such a thing could happen. He threw up his hands, shook his head in disbelief, and sighed: 'And there's us falling out with neighbours over politics, and those fellows up in Dublin having lunch together.'

There was a strong Republican element along the border, which occasionally surfaced. Paddy Cole's grandfather, Peter Hughes, was a scutcher and worked in a scutching mill 12 miles outside Castleblaney. The mill was owned by a man named Pakie Keenan who came into 'Blaney for a few pints on Saturday nights. Having drunk more than enough, Pakie would emerge on to the main street at closing time and shout an open invitation to all and sundry: 'Is there a man among you who will come with me and we'll take the border?'

'As a very young boy,' says Cole, 'I used to wonder where he was taking the border!'

Indeed, so relaxed were relations with the British army that many young musicians joined the British army in Armagh. This was a common occurrence at the time and many fine musicians did their apprenticeship in Armagh.

'It shows you the relaxed atmosphere of the time, and that feelings were not at all as bad as people sometimes believe.'

Even as a young boy growing up in the 1940s, Paddy Cole was aware of the huge difference in the standards of living when he crossed the Border into Armagh.

'As soon as you crossed, you saw the magnificent houses and the high standard of the roads. It was like going into an English town. But I also noticed there were neglected areas there, too, like South Armagh, which was predominantly Catholic, and was largely ignored for Government funding.

The main source of employment in Castleblaney was Mc Elroy's furniture factory and McAree's shoe factory.

In the evenings after school Paddy Cole, like most other young lads, went up to McElroy's factory to buy bags of waste wood for the fire. After school he also worked for a couple of hours selling petrol at a local garage owned by Isaac Hillis.

'Isaac had a sweet shop too, and on Saturday night I would have to wait until all the hackney car-drivers had been paid for my money. He might just decide to give me a bag of sweets instead of money. But of course, if I went home with just a bag of sweets I was in big trouble with my parents. They thought I had asked for the sweets instead.'

Paddy Cole has many happy memories of Isaac Hillis. 'He used to warn me that when I learned to drive, to always drive at a speed that I could stop if there was a crash around the next corner. He was a great big man, who wore a huge soft hat, and we thought he was like God Almighty.'

Summer time was spent playing around the Hope Estate and fishing for pike and perch from a hanging bridge on Lake Muckno.

'I also played football in the wee field behind the house in Lakeview with fellows like Ollie Mooney, PJ Hanratty — all great footballers. And we used to hunt with dogs.

'To this day I can remember the names of the dogs, which makes my mother think I'm cracking up. There was "Prince" Hearty, "Spot" Walsh, "Speed" O'Connor, "Bruce" McDonald, "Dinky" Finnegan, and our own "Rover" Cole. These hunting trips were organised by Pakie Connor, and for some strange reason he called his two dogs 'Síle'.

Some of Paddy's earliest memories are of his father practising the saxophone in the kitchen, and of cars pulling up in the evening to collect him for gigs. He would return home in the early hours to get a short sleep before rising again at the crack of dawn to go to the day job, driving the mail van. His job was to drive to a place called Aughnamullen to deliver the mail, spend a few hours there before bringing back mail to 'Blaney. In Aughnamullen, he rested in the home of an elderly lady, Ms Marron, who had come home from New York to retire. He would often bring his son with him on the run.

'Susan Marron used to tell us about a huge house she worked in as a maid in New York, many years before. In the evenings, when she felt lonely, she used to walk along by the banks of the Hudson River. Little did I know that years later I would often walk along by the same Hudson River when on a trip to the States, and think of Susan Marron and what she had told me.'

Paddy Cole Snr kept his fishing rods at the Marron house for fine weather, and his saxophone for the wet days.

'If the weather was bad, we would get in some practice on the saxophone, or in fine weather we'd go fishing and I used to love that. My father taught me everything about wildlife. We saw squirrels, rabbits and badgers and spent many hours together watching animals.'

Many years later Paddy was delighted to bring his father on one of his many trips to America.

During the visit Paddy Cole Snr had some postcards to send home, and asked an armed officer where was the nearest post office. The tense, burly officer, who was overseeing the arrival of a large cash consignment, turned abruptly, and snapped at him: 'Get to fuck out of here, Buddy!'

Paddy Cole Snr was having none of it, took the officer's number and started a heated argument. Eventually his son had to drag him away.

One of the postcards Paddy Cole Snr had written was to his old friend of many years, Leo Collins, a fine sax player from Crossmaglen, who played football with Armagh. However, when Mr Cole returned home to Ireland, he was devastated to hear that Leo Collins had died in the meantime.

Years before Collins had returned from Croke Park, having played a in a match for Ulster. Paddy Cole Snr greeted him on the following day: 'Hey, Leo, you played very well yesterday.'

'Oh, wait 'till you hear this, Paddy,' says Leo. 'I was marching around Croke Park behind the Artane Boys Band and this lad in front of me was playing a Sellmer Mk 6, and you should hear the sound he was getting out of it.'

Leo had become totally absorbed in the saxophone even though he was about to play a major game for Ulster.

Early school days for Paddy Cole and his six sisters were at the local Convent of Mercy, where he was taught by Sister Columba and Sister Pius. Discipline was strict and Mae Cole, Paddy's sister, remembers being sent out the town to buy a cane with which to be punished. The embarrassment of walking down the street with the cane was part of the punishment.

'If we were late back from home after lunch, we got a slap of the cane across each hand,' she recalls.

Being the only boy, Paddy was spoiled by his mother, though she denies it. He was, for example, the only member of the family who was allowed to have his vegetable soup strained at dinner! A regular desert for the family was tapioca, but young Cole hated it.

'He used to rush in the door shouting: "No tapioca for Paddy today", Mae recalls. 'Eventually it became a sort of password for him.'

Being the only boy also meant that he had his own bedroom from an early age, a fact resented by his sisters. The special relationship between mother and son continued into Paddy's career, and is as strong today as it was then.

When he reached third class, Paddy transferred to the Boys' National School where he met some exceptional teachers — the headmaster, Tom Hardy, Master O'Toole and Master McDonnell. Eamon O'Toole was a Tipperary man, who grew up in Thurles. He taught in Castleblaney for 18 years before moving to Dublin, where he now lives in retirement. Both Master Hardy and Master O'Toole were very musical.

'We did a lot of choir work,' recalls Paddy. 'It was tedious work for teachers, trying to get us to learn seconds and thirds and not just the melody. Some of the tunes I can still remember because of the intense practice.

'But Master O'Toole instilled a great love of choirs in us and a real appreciation of music. We learned songs like *How Keen The Delight of the Huntsman*? and *Row Boatman, Row.* I remember one boy in the class, Peter Donoghue, a huge big fellow and all through the song he just went: *Row...row....row...row.* He had an easy line!'

Relaxing in his home in the Templeogue, Eamon O'Toole still remembers his pupil of the late 1940s and early '50s.

'Paddy was easily the best boy in the class. He was very bright. We used to do two-part songs but once, when Master Hardy was away on sick leave, we tried a few three-part pieces, which was really something in a three-teacher national school. You could not depend on young children to stay in tune, but Paddy Cole would carry a whole part by himself. Sometimes, if Paddy was absent, I would say to the class: "We'll skip the singing class today because Paddy Cole is not here."'

Despite their high standard, the school choir gave few public performances other than the occasional appearance at the local Lyric Theatre, and a one-off trip to Monaghan Town to take part in liturgical plain chant. The singing was not without its lighter moments.

At Christmas time the choir went around the town with the carol singers. One lad, who could not sing a note, Raymond Dignam, went because his mother, Maggie, used to give him five shillings whenever he appeared. He couldn't sing, so he just mimed all the time to collect the money.

Pupils of the Convent of Mercy National School in Castleblaney. Paddy Cole is fifth from left in the middle row. Sally McKenna who played with Paddy in his first band is fourth from right in back row.

It was many years later that Eamon O'Toole went to see his former pupil play at a charity concert in the National Stadium in Dublin in 1992. While Paddy was waiting to go on stage he nudged his trumpet player and fellow 'Blaney man, Neilus McKenna: 'Look who's here, Neilus. It's Master O'Toole!'

'It made us nervous that Master O'Toole was there watching us,' says the former pupil. After all those years we still called him "Master".'

Apart from learning music, Paddy Cole played football for the school team and some minor football for the Faughs club.

'One day I was playing against Ballybay when I got a thump in the lip. It was split open and swelled up. I was supposed to be playing at a gig that night in Latton Hall, but I had to pull out and lose the 10/-. Straight away I hung up the football boots!

When the new boys' school opened, Paddy Cole was selected to read the welcoming address to the Bishop of Clogher, Dr Eugene O'Callaghan. The address was in Irish and Paddy memorised ever word. Paddy's sister, Carmel, remembers that a special brown corduroy suit was bought for the occasion and photographed for posterity!

After primary school, it was on to the local Vocational School for the teenager Cole. He showed a great aptitude for Irish and won a few scholarships to Teach Peadar Gallagher in the Ranafast Gaeltacht in Donegal. Sometimes he declined the offer, having already set up a summer job for himself — with good earning potential — with Isaac Hillis, plus some sax playing with the Maurice Lynch Band. He did sit the Fáinne exams, and returned to 'Blaney the proud owner of a sparkling gold ring.

In the Vocational School one of his teachers was a newly qualified man from Sligo, Phil Giblin.

'I remember Paddy and his class very well because they were my first senior class as a young teacher, and I was aware I was being sized up by them,' recalls Giblin, who now teaches in the Comprehensive School in Cootehill.

One evening as Phil Giblin was fixing an electrical socket, Paddy Cole and a couple of class mates, Tommy Duffy and Pat Finn, arrived on the scene. Suddenly, for a prank, Finn jumped up on the teacher's back.

A young Paddy Cole reads the welcoming address to the Bishop of Clogher, Dr Eugene O'Callaghan at the opening of the new boys' National School in Castleblaney.

Phil Giblin was having none of it. He quickly dislodged the student and having disciplined him, approached his now open-mouthed companions, Cole and Duffy.

'Well lads, do any of you want to try anything else on?' he enquired.

'Er...No...Sir!' replied an obedient Cole.

The Maurice Lynch 'wagon' often picked up the enthusiastic young sax player outside 'Blaney Vocational School, heading off to Dublin to play at dances in the Olympic Ballroom.

Cole took a year off secondary school to sample the hard outside world of earning a living. He went to work in Mallon's butcher's shop on Main Street.

'The family had a long tradition in butchering and I became familiar with all aspects of the trade, from the killing right through to the sausage-making. Johnny McAdam worked there with me and he still works for young Frank Mallon, one of the beef barons in the country. It was a great experience. '

Cole also worked for part of the year with Willie McAuley — father of Leslie McAuley, the MD of Norish Foods — on the electrification of Co. Monaghan.

But a lack of sleep, resulting from the previous night's gig with the Maurice Lynch band, sometimes meant that the young Cole was not as alert on the job as he ought to have been:

'Out in the house of local Fine Gael politician, Arthur Carvill, we put in some extra switches. While wiring the dairy, Jackie Doherty told me to put in a fuse to test the current. I walked back to my job and foolishly grabbed the ends of the two wires I was working on.

'The next thing I remember was wakening up on the far side of the dairy among a heap of milk cans. Luckily enough the current had thrown me. If I had stuck to it, I would have been stone dead. I was so tired from being out at night that I was not thinking properly.'

But the work had its spin-off benefits too.

'We wired Benny Campbell's house outside Castleblaney, and I stalled as long as I could because there were five or six daughters in the house, all smashers!

'Then there was an old man, Harry Farmer, living on his own, who used to insist on frying bacon and eggs for us. If he hadn't told us what it was, we would never have recognised it. There was this black object hanging out of the rafters, and suddenly we saw where it was sliced clean. It was a side of bacon. We used to put the food in our pockets rather than eat it.'

Another big musical influence on Paddy Cole was Tipperary man, Christy McCarthy, who played the trumpet with The Regal Dance Band, in Castleblaney. After tea, a few evenings a week, Paddy Cole would pack his saxophone and haul it across the town to Christy McCarthy's flat, where the former RAF musician would put him through the various orchestrations.

'It was music, music, non-stop in Christy's flat,' says Paddy. 'Both he and his brother Johnny, who played the trombone, were terrific musicians. Christy was a great help in teaching me to read music at the time. I remember coming home in the evenings with pieces of music like *Song of India*, and my father would say: 'You're into the heavy stuff, now, son".'

'I knew Paddy, his father and the whole family,' McCarthy remembers. 'I started my own band and I asked him along with others for a blow. I took out these orchestrations but they hadn't a bull's notion what they were about. Bit by bit, over a period of a few months, we got the whole thing together. Paddy was only playing the alto sax at that time, I think it was a plastic one at first.'

'Christy McCarthy had the patience of a saint,' says Cole. 'I remember he had his own band, "The Christy McCarthy Band", and one year we all went down to Tipperary town on holidays. There we met musicians like Slim Callaghan, and his brother Timmy, and Mick Tuohy. I don't know what we sounded like, but Christy was the anchor man in the band and kept it going.'

'In Tipperary, we used to go into Horkan Fitzgerald's teashop at Kickam Place,' says Christy McCarthy. 'But all the girls were knocking on the window looking in at these fellows in jeans, and we got barred. It was the first time I was barred from anywhere, and in my own town.'

While in Tipperary, Christy McCarthy was booked for a a gig for a boxing club in County Cork.

'When Paddy's mother heard we were going to Cork, she wouldn't let him because there was some sort of epidemic in the city at the time. Paddy cried a lot and eventually we persuaded his mother to let him go. And, of course at that time Paddy Cole was not allowed to sing with the band.'

'On the way back to Castleblaney, Cole said he would like to drive the car, a Morris Oxford, which had seven passengers and equipment.

'We were all tired and fell asleep while Cole drove away. Around Navan I woke up to the strange smell of burning rubber. Cole, then 16, had driven up the whole way with the handbrake on. He had hardly ever driven a car before.'

Cole travelled with The Christy McCarthy Band to the West. The crew of eight stopped in Edgeworthstown, Co. Longford where the driver was seen to have a few glasses.

'Outside Balinalee, the car came to a bend, but the driver didn't,' says McCarthy. 'Over we went.'

The roof rack, with all the equipment went straight off into a field. The car ended up sideways in a foot of water.

'We were bruised and shaken but not badly injured,' says Cole. Later in the night we were playing a Latin American number. I picked up the tambourine, and discovered it was covered in cow shit! The smell was desperate, but the gig always came first, and we played anyway.'

The following day McCarthy and a friend arrived back to the scene, turned the car back on its wheels, and drove out of the field.

Some years earlier one of Paddy Cole's first ventures into showbands was in a threesome band with Sally McKenna — his first girlfriend, according to reliable sources — and her cousin, Kevin McKenna. Paddy played saxophone, Sally the accordion, and Kevin, drums.

'On reflection I'd say the sound was pretty unique,' laughs Paddy. 'Imagine the Glen Miller sax section of one sax player of 12 years of age. The mind boggles, but we did it. Sometimes we had to take the battery out of the car to operate the amplifier. The guy who drove us had to get a quid for that. Many a time we played with no amplification . . . . for six hours!

'People told us we were great and even then, as a youngster, I tried to get more money where I could. We were on £5 a night in Oram Hall, and I went along to Paddy McGeogh, a senior member of the management committee, and asked for an extra pound. Paddy consulted his committee and came back and agreed, but he insisted the dance would now be from 9p.m. to 3a.m. instead of 2a.m. An extra hour for a pound, but we did it.'

The group also played in Tullynahinra hall, frequented by a family from Laragh, Co Monaghan, with a reputation for trouble.

'They were tough guys and one night, coming up to 2a.m. Peter Coleman and a gang arrived and would not let us finish. "You'll call the last dance when I tell you to call it," he warned me, before locking the doors. We were so terrified that we kept playing.'

Today Sally McKenna smiles when she remembers the days with the teenage band.

'I don't ever remember a time when I did not know Paddy Cole,' says Sally, who now lives in Malahide. 'We used to play at Macra dos and at fund-raising events for schools. We used to play numbers like *In the Mood*, *Little Brown Jug*, and *Tuxedo Junction*.

'The band went for a few years. I remember I was doing my Intermediate Certificate and the nuns were not happy. They were not as liberal as they are nowadays. Our average age was only 15, and we were billed as "the youngest jazz band in Ulster".'

Paddy was the one of the most professional people she has ever met, she says.

'He is innately musical, right through to his bones. He always makes it look so easy. That's the true professional. I've never heard anyone say: "Ah, he wasn't as good as he normally is." Every performance is one hundred per cent.'

2
I CAN'T SING AND I HAVE THE RECORDS TO PROVE IT!

The Castleblaney of the 1950s was a very musical town. Although small, the area boasted many well-known bands — The Regal, The Maurice Lynch Band, The Emmett Ceili Band, Pat McGuigan's band, Coogan's Stradella Dance Band, The John Murphy Dance Band and, much later, The Mainliners.

The best known was The Regal, which was run by Sean Farrell. Paddy Cole Snr played sax with the band for many years before joining Maurice Lynch. His brother, Phil, was the band's drummer and an early idol for Paddy Cole, who originally had started to learn the drums.

'Phil Farrell used to have a large kit of drums set up above his mother's confectionery shop in Castleblaney and I remember calling up to the shop to find out at what time my father was being collected. I remember going upstairs and Phil put me sitting behind this huge kit of drums, and I was so frightened I froze. At home all I had at the time was a little snare drum on a chair.

'My father was disgusted when he heard this because he used to be telling the lads in the band how good I was at the drums. Phil blew the whistle on me.'

The Regal Danceband from Castleblaney, Back row: (from left) Jack McManus (bass), Phil Farrell (drums), Pat Donaghue (accordion), Sadie Loughman (piano). Front row: Sean Farrell (sax), Paddy Cole Snr (sax), Frank Gormley (violin), Frank McArdle (trumpet) and Christine McManus (vocals).

Old Mick Coogan was the driving force behind Coogan's Stradella Band. One night, returning from a dance in an old Ford which he was driving himself, a lot of steam started to hit the windscreen.

'Mick, where's all that steam coming from?' asked one of the boys in the back.

'I don't know,' said Mick. 'It only started when when we went under that last bridge.

'What bridge?' asked the boys in the back. 'There's no bridge on this road.'

They stopped and got out to discover the bonnet had blown off the engine!

In the mid-1950s, the biggest dancehall draw of all was The Clipper Carlton, a band that came together almost by accident, and which was to point the way for a myriad of showbands for the next 20 years.

In his book *Send 'Em Home Sweatin*, Vincent Power a journalist with *The Cork Examiner,* recounts how the Strabane band lit the fuse that led to the showband explosion of the '60s by putting a show into their nightly routine.

'It was known as *Juke Box Saturday Night*. While orchestras provided the musical accompaniment for the dance floor, the Clippers became the centre of attention. They became entertainers, wore colourful suits, got rid of the music stands and moved around the stage. The Clippers transformed the dancing ritual simply by becoming themselves.'

While the idea of getting rid of the music stands sounds like a very simple idea now, it was a risky step at the time. But it worked. The band drew thousands to any venue they played, north or south of the Border. Their music knew no political or religious differences. The band was as popular in Cork as in Belfast.

'The Clipper Carlton stood up and performed, put a show into the dance band business, and added razzamatazz,' wrote journalist Sam Smyth, who was involved in the entertainment scene in Belfast. 'They began playing popular tunes from the hit parade, imitating the latest records heard on Radio Luxembourg, making jokes on stage, and looking as if they were enjoying themselves . . . . The Clipper Carlton were part of the new order as Ireland caught up with a world creeping away from post-Second World War sameness and shortages.'

The earnings of the band were huge in comparison with average wages at the time. Managed by Navan man Maxi Muldoon, they were the first to demand a percentage of the door rather than taking a straight fee. At 50% of an average crowd of 2,500 at 5/- a head, their fee was £312, the equivalent of about

£5,000 in today's terms. By the early '60s some of the Irish showbands were among the best paid in the world.

The Clippers got their name by chance. Having started out as Hugh Tourish and his band, they played regularly at the Palladrome Ballroom in Strabane every Saturday night.

'There was a dance one night in Fintona, outside Armagh,' Maxi Muldoon recalls. 'The band ran a competition for a name. A woman who never claimed the prize came up with The Clipper Carlton.'

The Clipper Carlton band from Strabane: Fergie O'Hagan (bass), Victor Flemming (trombone), Art O'Hagan (guitar), Hugo Quinn (trumpet), Terry Logue (sax) and Micky O'Hanlon (drums).

The name conjured up images of transatlantic travel. At the time all Pan American flying boats passing through Foynes, as well as land craft passing through Shannon, were known as Clippers. The most famous flying boat was the Yankee Clipper.

The line-up of The Clippers was: Hugo Quinn, trumpet; Hugh Tourish, piano; Terry Logue, sax and clarinet; Micky O'Hanlon, drums; Art O'Hagan vocals and double bass; and his brother Fergus, MC and vocals.

In 1954 Victor Flemming joined the band, playing trombone and piano. That was the year they abandoned the orchestral chairs for good, and took to their feet.

The Clippers were unique. They had their own custom-built wagon and even their own stamps printed.

There were other highly professional bands from the North, including The Melotones from Belfast and Dave Glover.

'Ernie Watson was a sax player with The Melotones and used to give me a lot of help with the music,' says Paddy Cole. 'I can remember he used to live in Jennings Park, Belfast, because I would write to him there. On reflection, I probably annoyed him with all the queries, queries, queries.

'I remember Dave Glover playing in The Embassy Hall in 'Blaney early one night in front of maybe one hundred people. He was trying to get the dancing started, always a difficult task. Dave shouted down: "Come on lads, there's some beautiful girls here. Come and get them on the floor. One of the girls shouted back: "Why don't you do it?" With that he put down his trumpet and came down off the stage and started dancing.'

There were other bands, too who made a major impact in Castleblaney.

'The Black Aces from Kilkenny and Johnny Flynn from Tuam used to pack the halls. Johnny Flynn had top class musicians. Frankie Hannon and Danny Kelly who was later killed in a car crash. The Melody Aces from Newtownstewart were a huge draw in our town. Shay Hutchinson was their lead singer, and they had what I would term a country band with brass. Their leader was John Devine, and after a gig on a Wednesday he used to say to Sean Mulligan, the owner of the old Embassy ballroom in 'Blaney: "Mr Mulligan, that was as good as a Sunday night", in the hope of getting a few extra quid. The Swingtime Aces came from Galway and people around the country still talk about them.'

When the young Paddy Cole finished school in 'Blaney the local garda boss, Sgt Muldoon, wanted him to join the force because he was over six feet in height and spoke fluent Irish. Cole declined.

'I was offered a job in McElroy's furniture factory for 10/- a week which was the norm, but I suddenly realised all I wanted to do was play music, and so I opted for The Maurice Lynch Band where I could earn £1.10/- a night.'

Cole, like everyone else, came under the influence of The Clipper Carlton.

'The band came on the scene around that time, and they were a huge influence on guys of my age.'

Another major influence was The Johnny Quigley Band from Derry.

'I remember going to see them one night in Dundalk. The musicians took a five minute break halfway through. They had been playing in dress suits but suddenly came back on in mad green jackets. The chairs were dispensed with and they put on a whole new show, choreography, the lot.'

There was a huge musical tradition in Derry. Soon they city was to produce Phil Coulter, who was to become closely identified with The Capitol Showband. The music scene in Derry had been boosted by the presence of US servicemen since the Second World War, who were spending money and demanding to hear the popular music they left behind. They had records mailed to them which were picked up by local bands and copied on stage.

It was in Dundalk that the young Paddy Cole first laid eyes on another famous band, The Mick Delahunty Orchestra from Clonmel.

'In my early band days a special mouthpiece, called a "Brilhart", came out, which had a very good reputation. My mother gave me the money to buy it and I went to Machett's shop in Belfast. I didn't like it and had some difficulty getting my money back.

'I went to hear Mick Delahunty in the Town Hall in Dundalk. We arrived in late in our wagon and for devilment Maurice Lynch sent up an anonymous request for *The Carnival of Venice*, a famous trumpet solo. It was the end of the night and the band would already have been blowing for six hours, but Benny McNeill — now in the National Concert Orchestra — played it perfectly.

'Later I spoke to Mick Del and asked him about the mouthpiece. Although not knowing who I was, he put his hand in his case, took out the mouthpiece and gave it to me.

"Take it with you, and if you like it send me on a few quid. If you don't just send it back."

'I liked it and sent on £7 to Mick Del in Clonmel. I got a letter back from his wife saying he was delighted. I always remember the incident because Mick Delahunty did not have a clue who I was.

'Maurice Lynch was one of the best entertainers and showmen I ever knew. On stage, he had a great sense of humour which came across to the crowd. Even before the advent of The Clipper Carlton, he had us standing up for the second half of the show.'

The vocalist in the band was Tommy Toal, who would sit in full dress suit at the side of the stage while waiting to sing.

The full band line-up was: Maurice Lynch, trumpet and accordion; Francy Leonard, trumpet; Micky O'Neill, sax; Paddy Cole Snr and Paddy Cole Jnr, sax; Peter Hickey, sax; Gerry Duffy, trombone; Gerry Muldoon, guitar; Petie Lynch, bass; Charlie Lynch, drums, Attracta Lynch, piano and Eileen Lambe, vocals. The line-up changed from time to time, depending on the particular circumstances. Later they were joined by Neilus McKenna on trumpet (still with The Paddy Cole Band), Charlie McCoy, vocals, and Johnny Beatty on piano. Beatty later joined The Mainliners, creating the unique organ sound that became synonymous with the band.

Carmel Cole, Paddy's sister, remembers The Maurice Lynch wagon calling to their home in the evening to collect her father and brother.

'The arrival of the wagon outside often meant that the Rosary was cut short, and we escaped all the trimmings, which were as long as the Rosary itself! Maurice Lynch would come in, kneel down and say the last decade with us. The Rosary was always recited in our home no matter what the hurry', she recalls.

Members of the Maurice Lynch Band. Back row: (from left) Paddy Cole Jnr, Peter Hickey (sax). Third row: John Beatty (piano), Frankie Lynch (drums), Micky O'Neill (sax). Second row: Maurice Lynch (trumpet), Gerry Muldoon (guitar), Audie Heaney (vocals). Front row: Paddy Cole Snr (sax).

For the musician it was tough going, on the road up to six nights per week.

'The ballrooms were pretty basic,' says Paddy. 'They put up four walls with a roof overhead, and they added a "telephone kiosk" for the band to change in. Some of the halls did not even have electricity in the early days. Instead, they used tilly lamps, in Oram Hall for example, and when the lights darkened, the caretaker, Paddy McGeough, would go around and pump up the lamps in case the lads got a bit too amorous with the ladies.

'The dust was also dreadful on some of those old wooden floors, and they used to throw paraffin on them to keep it down. The smell would knock you. They also scraped candles on the floor to make them slippery. Nobody had heard of personal injury claims in those days.'

Suddenly ballrooms mushroomed all over the country. Associated Ballrooms, established in 1964, and comprising three of the best known men in the business — Con Hynes, Jack O'Rourke and Donie Collins — owned 30 ballrooms, including some of the biggest in the land, such as The Talk of the Town in Galway and The Majestic in Mallow. In Longford, Albert Reynolds and his brother Jim built The Cloudland in Rooskey and went on to own a 14 ballroom chain, stretching as far south as Limerick.

Other independent operators slotted into any gap in the chain. These included The Oyster in Dromkeen, Co Limerick, owned by Pakie Hayes; The Golden Vale in Dundrum, Co Tipperary, owned by Austin Crowe, The Redbarn in Youghal and The Stardust in Cork City, owned by the Lucey Brothers, Murt and Jerry; McIvor's ballroom in Muff, Co Donegal, and Sean Byrne's Strandhill ballroom in Sligo.

'Sean Byrne's father,' says Cole, 'was a big guy, who had lived all his life in England and everybody called him "Daddy" Byrne, even the bands. Another son, Patsy Byrne was a great lad for devilment. When old "Daddy" Byrne, used to do bread deliveries, Patsy would run over and unzip his fly while he was carrying the hot bread on big trays over his head. He had to keep walking while shouting "Go 'way you bastard" at his son!

'Strandhill was a favourite meeting point for musicians from both sides of the Border. Jazz sessions were held there regularly after dances.

'Invariably we finished up going to bed at five or six in the morning, and then had to get up to start rehearsing again. The place was like a home from home for us.'

In Castleblaney Sean Mulligan built The Embassy ballroom, now the site of The Glencarn Hotel, which still retains some of the old ballroom walls. (In building the hotel, construction workers came across one piece of graffiti which read: "Paddy Cole courted a woman against this wall".)

The Embassy became a star attraction for dancing fans within a 50-mile radius. 'I can remember playing there on a Wednesday night to crowds of 1,500 to 1,600. It was unbelievable the crowds that were going to these places. These days The Glencarn, owned by Monaghan man Mick Sherry, is still drawing in the crowds.'

The Maurice Lynch Band frequently travelled to Dublin for gigs and were particularly popular in Waterford. They were regulars at the famous "Ags" dances in The Olympic in Dublin run by a Committee that, ironically, included two members of the future Capitol Showband, Des Kelly and Eamon Monaghan.

'I remember Des Kelly once coming to Maurice Lynch and telling him the band was the biggest draw they had, and quietly advising him to ask for more money. But because of the constant insecurity of the business Maurice did not increase the fee.'

Later the band ventured out to The Ritz Ballroom in Ballyfermot, run by Eddie Downey. There the reception from the Dubs was a bit more hostile. The gig in Ballyfermot was a tough one for a country band, but Eddie Downey was just as tough.

'I often remember seeing him carry two thugs out of the hall, one under each arm — and bang their heads off the swinging doors to open them on the way out. Eddie took no prisoners. But it was dog rough,' says Cole.

'Go home ye culchies,' the crowd would roar at The Maurice Lynch Band, demanding that popular local Dublin bands such as The Blue Clavons, who included Butch Moore in their number, be brought on.

'However, we eventually won them over with skiffle numbers and Elvis Presley medleys,' says Paddy, 'but it was not easy for a young lad.'

It was in The Ritz in Ballyfermot that Paddy Cole first noticed a young, but very professional master of ceremonies, by the name of Gay Byrne.

'Gay used to introduce the bands on stage. I noticed how professional he was even then. When we arrived, he was always there in a smart jacket, pair of slacks and a bow-tie.'

A priest called Fr Brendan Heffernan, now a parish priest in Portmarnock, but then a curate in Ballyfermot, had asked a friend of Gaybo's, Brendan O'Gorman, to help with some fund-raising.

'At the time,' Gay Byrne remembers, 'we used to do a double act in pantomimes and shows, and Fr Heffernan was given The Ritz ballroom every Tuesday night at a special rate. I think we were there for a couple of years.'

Many years later Paddy recorded a tune called *Bourbon Street Parade*, at the suggestion of RTE's Equestrian Correspondent, Brian MacSharry, then a DJ with Downtown Radio.

'I took the record into RTE myself and I was walking down a corridor when I saw *The Gay Byrne Show* on a door. I knocked and a girl emerged. In the distance, I could see Gaybo with his head down at a desk, but I did not ask for him. Instead I said to the girl: "If Gay thinks this is good enough, he might give it a spin. If not, then tell him to throw it in the bin."

'The girl laughed at me. But Gay must have liked it, because he gave it a few plays and it helped.'

The showband days had their wild side, with drink, women and fast cars all constant hazards. The bands often fell victim to one, two or all three!

One regular casualty was guitarist Gerry Muldoon, a wild young man in a hurry. Nicknamed 'Red Alert' by Maurice Lynch, he was known to have 'written off' several cars through speeding.

He was once hit by a train in a VW beetle while crossing a railway line, but survived against the odds! Propped up in plaster in a hospital bed, a colleague asked him about his thoughts as he was being dragged along for a hundred yards by the train.

'I thought I would be exchanging the guitar for a harp,' he quipped.

'On another occasion,' says Paddy, 'Gerry drove straight into a solid cement drinking-trough for horses in the centre of Dublin and was badly injured. Back in hospital, I remember him complaining that he would have to pay for the damage to the trough!'

If it wasn't cars, it was woman trouble. After a dance in Barry's Hotel one summer, Gerry Muldoon, drummer Frankie Lynch and Paddy Cole commandeered the band's wagon, and three women. The party went missing for several hours. Returning through O'Connell St they spotted an irate Paddy Cole Snr out looking for his son, and furious over the missing wagon as he had to be up early for work the next morning.

'Paddy's father was very angry and gave him a good hiding in the back of the wagon. It was difficult for Paddy having his father in the band on these occasions,' says Muldoon, who now works with the *Northern Standard* newspaper.

A favourite meeting point for a meal and a chat with other bands in Dublin was the Richmond Cafe near Portobello bridge (beside the present-day Gigs Place). All showbands referred to it as 'Molly's', after the lady who served there.

'There was more business done in Molly's, and more dates fixed than anywhere else,' says Paddy. 'When I say Molly looked after you, I mean she really looked after you. You'd walk in on a cold winter's night, and Molly would look at you and say: "Have you no scarf to wear on a night like tonight?"

'The place was a great novelty for us. We'd finish playing in Barry's Hotel for Liam Ryan — the first man to bring the band to Dublin — and drive right across the city just because this place was open and we would meet the other bands. I'd talk to other musicians about the make of saxophone they were playing, or about a new mouthpiece that had come on the market. I went to Molly's for years, even later on when I was with The Capitol.'

In the '60s, when the showbands were at their peak, musicians compared their latest sportscars at Molly's. Powerful, expensive cars were a status symbol. The merits of a six-cylinder Jaguar were measured against those of a top-of-the-range Merc.

Daybreak often saw a line-up of two or three powerful cars on top of Rathmines bridge to see who could reach the highest speed in the least time.

Molly died in 1994, but the tradition of late night stops is still carried on in the Gigs Place next door, now owned by Brian Carr, a former member of The Royal Blues.

The Maurice Lynch Band also toured England and Scotland. While in Glasgow, they got a booking from a promoter, Bill Fehilly, in the remote town of Wick. However, the journey proved a bit more difficult than they had anticipated because of the freezing snow. As a result the wagon pulled into Wick a full day late, but the gig went ahead anyway.

'The people of Wick thought we were some sort of entertainers,' says Gerry Muldoon. 'The only bands they had known were The Beatles and Chris Barber. We had a singer with us, Harry Mitchell from Belfast and he and Paddy did Elvis numbers. Paddy discovered a new opening and sang tunes like *Goodness Gracious Me*. The fans loved it and these songs became a regular part of the show.'

Harry Mitchell came from Belfast's Shankill Road.

'He was a fully committed loyalist, and we accepted that,' says Cole, 'but there used to be a lot of slagging about the Shankill and the Falls Road. I remember once, we were waiting to get on a boat in Liverpool and we went to the La Carno ballroom, part of the Mecca chain. Harry suddenly went up to the band leader and asked could he sing a few band numbers. The fellow was stunned that someone would come up in the middle of a packed crowd. But Harry was so good he was offered a job with the band there and then, but he came home with us. He just wanted to prove a point. He played with The Witnesses and later ended up in Spain where he subsequently died.

In Scotland The Maurice Lynch Band played for Frank O'Neill, who owned a club in Earl Street in the Gorbals. 'It was a rough club in Glasgow, frequented mostly by Donegal people from the

Rosses. The teddy boys were in at the time and the city was famous for these gangs. There used be vicious fights in the ballrooms. A gang would set on a bouncer before the others could get to him. It was a strange atmosphere in which to play happy '50s rock 'n' roll music.'

It was in Glasgow that Cole first met the footballer Pat Crerand, then playing with Glasgow Celtic.

'I remember once going to Mass with him down near the Gorbals and the kids crowded the seats just to get a look at him. He later went to Manchester United. He was a tough player, and the most accurate man with a ball that I have ever seen. He had a lot of Donegal connections.'

Cole had an uncle, Tim Hughes, in Glasgow.

Paddy Cole (left) on his way to the remote Scottish Isle of Stornaway with fellow members of the Maurice Lynch band, Frankie Lynch (drums) and Audie Heaney (vocals).

'I used to visit him and often we would go down to his local. I remember the white trench coats were in fashion at the time and I had bought one in the States, when on tour with The Capitol Showband. When we walked into the pub there was dead silence immediately.

"What's wrong, Tim?" I enquired.

"Say nothing,' he replied, before introducing me to the barman. Then the conversation struck up again.

'The crowd thought I was a police officer, or the "polis" as they would say.

By now Paddy Cole, the all-round entertainer had emerged.

'Very often the reason I was let sing on stage at all was because I was the only one who knew the particular words of a song. As I often say, I can't sing, and I have records to prove it!'

3
A RELIEF BAND CALLED THE BEATLES

One night in early 1961, a tall, dark-haired figure entered through the back of Barry's Hotel on Dublin's Great Denmark St. to watch The Maurice Lynch Band on stage. His particular interest was the band's young sax and clarinet player.

Eamonn Monahan was already an established musician and founder member of The Capitol Showband. He had heard many times about the sax playing of Paddy Cole, and had earmarked him as a replacement for a musician who was leaving the band.

'I stood at the back of the hall and saw this fellow on the stage,' Eamonn recalls. 'I did not believe anybody could be as good as Paddy Cole. I remember I stood in awe of him for a while."

The Capitol Showband had emerged as a response to the huge popularity of The Clipper Carlton, and later The Royal Showband.

Like Derry in the North, there was a strong music tradition in Waterford, where bands like The Clipper Carlton and The Maurice Lynch Band were very popular. Royal piano player Gerry Cullen remembers listening, with his father, to *The Billy Cotton Bandshow* on BBC Radio One.

'It was real showband stuff ahead of its time in the early 1950s,' he remembers. 'They played all the hits of the time. I also remember going to see Chris Barber in The Arundel Ballroom.'

Launched in 1957, the Royal decided to incorporate the word 'showband' into its name. The popularity of their lead singer, Brendan Bowyer, saw the band shoot to fame in a short time. Gerry Cullen remembers being approached by two of the founding members, Jim Conlon and Michael Coppinger, who had played with The Harry Boland Band, to read a particular piece of music for them.

'They also asked me if I was interested in joining a new band,' says Cullen. 'The Royal then started up shortly afterwards with Tom Dunphy, Brendan Bowyer (originally as a trombonist), Charlie Matthews, Jim Conlon and myself. We had no trumpet player.

'Our first date in Dublin was in The Olympic Ballroom, and we said we couldn't go there without a trumpet player. So we asked Eddie Sullivan, who was playing with St Patrick's brass band, and he joined. I remember at his first gig with us in Waterford we had forgotten to rehearse the National Anthem, and he couldn't play it.'

The Royal hired a taxi, an old Ford V8, and set out for Dublin with the large bass and drums on the roof. The journey took five hours.

'We got very good publicity in the evening papers and we took off. Eventually we had to take a decision to go professional because the roads were not good and the journeys took a long time. I was earning 10s.6d a week working in a sports shop in Waterford, but I earned £5 a night with the Royal.'

The band's first professional date was in the Seapoint in Galway on Easter Sunday night, 1959.

'We were greatly influenced by The Clipper Carlton whom we had seen in Waterford and Tramore. At a certain point in the night the dancing stopped, and we put on a show. A lot of it was skiffle as Lonnie Donegan was big then. Bowyer was doing Elvis, which was unheard of at the time.'

The Royal's quick rise in popularity was seen in 1959 when English pop singer Terry Dean, who was Number One in the charts, came to play in Waterford. While Dean attracted a mere 60 people to the Arundel Ballroom on a Sunday night, The Royal entertained 2,500 fans in the nearby Olympia. The band was still only semi-professional.

Cycling home after the dance, Gerry Cullen recognised a gloomy Dean standing outside the Bridge Hotel at 3.30a.m.

'I went over and said to him: "You're Terry Dean. How'd the gig go tonight?"

"Forget it," replied Dean, "some bloody local band was playing nearby and blew us out of the water."'

The band's earning ability was boosted when they acquired a new manager, Carlow man TJ Byrne, who previously had sold everything from muck spreaders to musical instruments.

'He was a great man for marketing The Royal,' Albert Reynolds said of TJ Byrne. 'He introduced a whole lot of marketing skills that weren't apparent in the business.'

The band headed for the North.

'No one could quite figure out The Royal Showband from Waterford,' wrote journalist Sam Smyth. 'They were never as slick and polished as the northern innovators, but within a year they had become the biggest attraction in dance halls from Dungarvan to Donegal . . . . They played the usual popular songs from the hit parade, but Brendan Bowyer was quite unique. He was ungainly and awkward, a big fella from Waterford, who looked as though he would be happier sitting on a tractor than holding audiences spellbound centre-stage.'

The Royal specialised in doing an Elvis medley, with Bowyer gyrating like the king. 'It wasn't that he did it well,' says Smyth, 'but rather that a man of his size would do it all, which seemed to fascinate the audiences.'

During Lent the band went to England as all the ballrooms were closed in the Republic. TJ Byrne made a deal with the giant Mecca ballroom chain whereby The Royal would play one night in each of its ballrooms during Lent. On one St Patrick's Night, the fire brigade had to be called to hose away the masses of fans trying to get in to The Hammersmith Palais.

'We went to Liverpool and a little known band played relief to us before we went on stage in The Empire Theatre,' recalls Gerry Cullen. 'They were known as The Beatles. We heard all the numbers before they were recorded. I remember talking to Paul McCartney and John Lennon that night, and they could not believe we were going to tour America. They were two lovely lads, very sincere.'

The band's first real experience of a major concert was in 1962 when they played to a packed Royal Albert Hall in London. In 1963 they were the subject of a special documentary, *One Nighters*, based on a typical week with the band. The film was directed by Peter Collinson, then a producer in RTE. It was shot over a period of eight weeks, and went on to win a special award at both the Cork Film Festival and at Cannes.

'It was most unusual at the time for a band to make a film,' says Gerry Cullen. 'Some of the crowd scenes were shot at 3 or 4a.m. in The Ulster Hall in Belfast and in The Top Hat in Dun Laoghaire. When the film was released generally, none of us could walk down any street without being recognised.'

Collinson later went on to produce a number of highly successful films, including *The Italian Affair*, starring Michael Caine.

The band also formed part of a BBC 2 television feature on the then rise of the Shannon industrial region. *The Hucklebuck* was Number One in the Irish charts, and its inclusion in the programme made it a major hit in Britain.

One of the high spots for The Royal was their own show at New York's world famous Carnegie Hall.

Band members enjoyed the fame, and lived like kings. But the going was tough.

Fr Brian D'Arcy recalled that the two big talking points about The Royal when he was a young student, were their Mercedes wagon and the fact that Brendan Bowyer could leap over Tom Dunphy on stage.

Kerry-born promoter Bill Fuller took The Royal to the States and they played New York, Boston, Chicago and Philadelphia. In New York The Royal went to see Nat King Cole. Gerry Cullen remembers the scene in The Coco Co Bana, a single spotlight on a grand piano.

'Suddenly this beautiful velvet voice started to sing *This Is a Lovely Way to Spend an Evening*, but we couldn't see him as it was very dark. It was the first time we saw a radio mike, and he had started the number in the kitchen before walking out. Later The Royal had their picture taken with him.

'He told us he remembered being in Dublin and being interviewed on a radio programme about sausages (Donnellys). He knew the name of the manager in The Theatre Royal, which we didn't, as well as the name of the night porter in The Gresham, where he stayed, which we didn't either. He was a gentleman out and out. He was dead within a year of that show.'

Promoter Bill Fuller decided to try Vegas and put The Royal in touch with promoter Rocky Sennes. In Vegas The Royal secured a truck, amplifiers and drums and went up and down the Strip doing auditions.

'At 10.30a.m. the top booking agents would sit in certain places,' says Cole, 'and all new acts would do their piece. Rocky Sennes saw The Royal and remarked: "These guys are so versatile, they could make it."'

In Vegas the big stars, including Elvis, came in to see the Royal. The band spent six months of the year in Las Vegas for five years.

In 1962 they became the first band to record a single, *Come Down the Mountain, Katie Daly* sung by Tom Dunphy. It was recorded by EMI. A year later they shot to Number One in the Irish Top Ten with Brendan Bowyer's rendition of the Elvis Presley number, *Kiss Me Quick* But the tune that will always be associated with The Royal is *The Hucklebuck.*

Bowyer first heard it performed by The Clipper Carlton in The Olympia Ballroom in Waterford in the 1950s, and later heard the earlier traditional versions recorded by Louis Armstrong and Count Basey. Gerry Cullen remembers the day it was recorded in late 1964:

'We were over in St John's Wood in London recording an album for EMI. Studio time was precious and Cliff Richard and the Shadows were waiting to come in. The guy in charge, Wally Ridley said: "Guys, you got eight minutes left. Do a number and we might use it on the back of a single or something, but don't waste the time. We were all arguing, so I suggested we do *The Hucklebuck*. We did one take. Done. No balancing, nothing.

'About two weeks later a guy rang from EMI and said: "You know this *Hucklebuck* thing. You might have something there." They sent over a demo. Then we got the brainwave of putting the four girls up the front and starting a new dance craze. The rest is history.'

The Hucklebuck went straight into the charts and remained there for twelve weeks. The song took the country by storm. Dancers loved to watch Bowyer wriggle and twist to the new craze alongside the female dancers, dressed in polo-neck blouses, white skirts and white bobby socks.

The record also made Number One in Australia, Hong Kong, and Singapore even though The Royal had never been there. Such was its popularity that it entered the charts again in Ireland in 1976, when it was re-released, and it did so yet again in 1981.

The guiding light behind The Capitol Showband was Des Kelly from Galway, who, with his brother Johnny, played in bands throughout the West. Like The Coles in Monaghan, the family had its own band for a while, called Quicksilver. Des played the keyboards, Johnny was the drummer while their sister, Bernie, played bass and sang.

They were joined by a few others in an outfit which was steeped in traditional Irish music.

In 1959, Des Kelly moved to UCD to study Agricultural Science and the Quicksilver band disbanded. In Dublin he quickly got involved in the music scene with another Agriculture student, Eamonn Monahan, who in turn introduced him to trumpeter Paul Sweeney, then an art student.

'We used to play in a place called Tir Na nOg, which is now The Grafton Arcade,' Eamonn Monahan recalls. 'It was an old skating rink. We used to get 5/- a night playing relief to a fellow called Tommy Delaney.'

Monahan, like most musicians of the time, came from a very musical family. His sister, Noreen Thomas, is a well known classical pianist and a member of the board of examiners of the Royal Irish Academy. Eamonn's first love was, and still is, classical music.

'I still play a lot of Chopin and love it,' says Monahan, now running a very successful business in Dublin, "Elegant John" bathrooms.

Des Kelly, Eamonn Monahan and Paul Sweeney decided to put together a bigger band. 'Paddy Cole was already a bit of a legend as a musician and we had decided to try to get him in along with three others, Don Long, a trombonist, Jimmy Hogan, a guitarist, and Butch Moore on vocals.

'Jimmy Hogan and Butch were already with The Blue Clavons, the hugely popular Dublin band,' says Monahan. 'Jimmy Hogan was ahead of his time and could play the guitar when no one could. The idea was they would join up with myself on piano, Des Kelly on bass, Johnny on drums and Paul Sweeney on trumpet.'

Hogan accepted the offer from The Capitol first, and Butch Moore joined shortly afterwards. Butch Moore's real name was Seamus Moore, one of a family of five from Dublin's North Circular Road. His brother, Des, is a well known guitarist, who has performed in many major shows, including *Riverdance*. His nephew, Paul Moore, is a member of the Cafe Orchestra. As a boy, Butch sang soprano and tap-danced before joining a number of small bands around Dublin. Eventually he linked up with The Blue Clavons, the popular Dublin band which attracted record crowds to The Olympic Ballroom.

Having joined the Capitol in 1960, Moore and the members decided to remain semi-professional until they had tested the volatile musical waters of the showband industry. Everybody held on to their day job. Des Kelly and Eamonn Monahan continued to study agriculture, Johnny Kelly was studying medicine at UCG. They recruited Pat Loughman on trombone and Eddie Ryan on saxophone.

The band hit the road for five nights a week, playing without a break from 9p.m. to 2a.m. After the show, they got back into an old van and returned to Dublin, and straight to college. That night they were off again. Eventually Johnny Kelly quit his medical studies and moved to Dublin to join the band full-time.

The full line-up now was: Eamonn Monahan, piano; Des Kelly, bass; Johnny Kelly, drums; Butch Moore, rhythm guitar and vocals; Jimmy Hogan, lead guitar and banjo; Paul Sweeney, trumpet; Pat Loughman, trombone and Eddie Ryan, saxophone.

In early 1961, The Capitol Showband turned professional under the management of Jim Doherty.

'It was a difficult decision to make,' Des Kelly told *Spotlight* magazine. 'But something had to suffer. We began getting more and more dates and our studies were being neglected. Instead of being in the library, the boys were on a bandstand, playing their hearts out.

'So we had a long talk and we decided that it was either stop being musicians and get down to serious study, or give up the idea of a university education and turn professional. It was not really a choice. We had all been bitten by the showband craze and we just couldn't give it up. It was the wisest decision we ever made.'

However, two of the musicians, Eddie Ryan and Pat Loughman opted not to go full-time and had to be replaced. Loughman was a teacher and Eddie Ryan worked with the Gas Company. Loughman was replaced on trombone by Don Long from Cork, who had played with The Donie Collins band.

The band had earmarked Paddy Cole to replace Eddie Ryan on sax. But it was not an easy task, and several trips were made to Castleblaney by Des Kelly, Eamonn Monahan and Jim Doherty in an effort to recruit him. Paddy Cole had gone to see The Capitol in The Swan Park Hall in Monaghan Town having heard so much about them.

'They were very good and fresh,' he remembers.

When they finished the gig, they asked Paddy to blow a few tunes with them, and to join The Capitol.

'It was a bit embarrassing at the time, and there was some bad feeling because Maurice Lynch, with whom I was playing, knew the lads very well. He felt I was being poached out of the band.'

There was another, more pressing problem — Mrs Cole. Paddy's mother was not happy at the idea of her son going off to live in faraway Dublin with strange people. In her view, it had been much safer when he was in The Maurice Lynch Band with his father and living at home.

'The boys in The Capitol told my mother they would organise me in a nice flat in the city. But that only made things worse because her idea of a flat in Dublin was one of these Ballymun-like structures. There was a lot of tension in the house, and so I told the boys I would not be joining.'

At the same time, Paddy Cole was contacted by Pat Campbell, who had a band in Emyvale. Campbell promised to match The Capitol's offer in cash if he would join them.

There was also an offer from Jack Ruane's band in Ballina.

'Kevin McKenna had joined that band and I also heard about this fabulous trout river, the Moy. Jack's son, Judd Ruane, who owns The Riverboat in Ballina today, is one of the most underrated Dixieland trumpet players I know.'

The negotiating team from The Capitol did not give up. They thought the money being offered might be a problem, and they raised their offer from £25 a week to £30, not bad pay for a 21-year-old in the Ireland of 1961.

'Money was never the problem,' says Paddy. 'One day my mother was speaking to Mrs Leavy, who owned the local chemist's shop. She and the local doctor, Dr Healy, urged her not to let me miss the opportunity of The Capitol. To this day, Mrs Leavy watches my career with interest, and can always tell me when I have appeared on television.'

The tension continued, with Paddy Cole Snr wanting his son to take up the offer.

'By now the word had got out in the business that The Capitol were looking for a sax player and that I had turned it down. There was a lot of interest,' says Paddy. 'Joe McIntyre, the sax player from Derry, said he used to walk along O'Connell St. jumping six feet in the air, hoping someone would recognise him. He thought one of the requirements of the job was that you could jump six feet

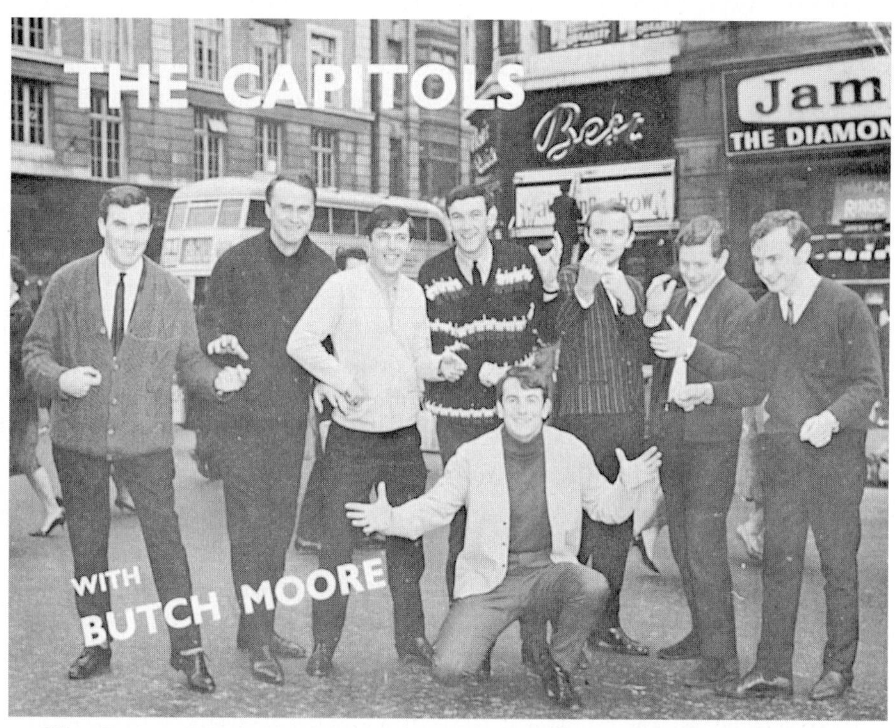

The Capital Showband pictured on Dublin's O'Connell Street. From Left: Des Kelly (bass guitar), Eamonn Monahan (piano) Jimmy Hogan (guitar and banjo) Paddy Cole (sax), Don Long (trombone), Brian McCarthy (trumpet), Johnny Kelly (drums). Front row: Butch Moore (vocals).

off the stage while holding your instrument intact! I recommended McIntyre for the job, as well as Gerry Rice, a sax player from Belfast and Jim McDermott from Derry.'

The negotiations continued.

'Paddy didn't have a car at the time and one of the things that finally persuaded Mrs Cole was that I would drive him to 'Blaney once a week,' says Eamonn Monahan. I remember I had a dark green Volkswagen at the time, ZW 4853.'

One of the people from whom Paddy sought advice on what he should do was his old teacher, Phil Giblin.

'He (Paddy) stopped me on the street one day and told me about the offer from The Capitol. I warned him this showband business could end very quickly, but if he joined, to invest some of his money in case he ended up with nothing. I also asked him not to forget his parents in 'Blaney.'

Finally the deal was signed, and Paddy Cole moved to the big smoke. Home in Dublin was a flat in 17 Botanic Road, Glasnevin, which he shared with Capitol drummer Johnny Kelly.

'Monday was our day off so we went out and bought steak and onions. Then it was out on the town. I didn't take a drink at the time, and a night out for us was to go to the pictures with some girlfriends.'

The Capitol took off very quickly with the new line-up, which included Paddy Cole and Don Long.

Promoters like Jim Aiken, Barney Curley, Malachy O'Neill, Peter Prendergast, Sean Byrne from Sligo, Bill Kenny from Waterford and the Lucey brothers from Cork came to listen, and booked them for months ahead.

Eamonn Monahan remembers one particular night playing relief to the Royal Showband in The Arcadia in Bray, before Cole or Don Long had joined up.

'When The Royal came on stage, the students started to jeer them and the story hit the papers. The headlines speculated that this was the new band that was going to take over from The Royal. But we never did take over.'

Later it was widely rumoured that the jeering had been organised. Royal keyboard player Gerry Cullen says there was 'friendly rivalry' between the two bands.

'Musically The Capitol were probably a better band. They could play Dixieland jazz, but we couldn't. We tried it but it didn't work. The Capitol were probably a bit ahead of their time, but we had the name and the pulling power.'

Cork was a tough nut to crack for any showband. The reason was The Dixies, Cork's own top class band. They were the resident relief band in The Arcadia Ballroom and had become extremely professional. They had their own in-built comedian, drummer Joe McCarthy, who indulged in endless stage antics. They never took themselves too seriously.

Returning from gigs around the country they were known to have stopped and marched down boreens playing trumpet and sax for cattle at 4a.m.! Joe Mac and guitarist Steve Lynch once caused confusion among a group of nuns at Cork railway station by playing a recording of the Angelus at 4.30 in the afternoon!

When The Dixies heard a 'big name' band was coming to The Arcadia, they put on a special effort — to put it up to the visitors. Joe Mac would be even funnier. Steve Lynch would hang out over the rails of the 10 ft high stage while playing *Guitar Boogie Shuffle* upside down.

'The Dixies are something of a phenomenon, reported *Spotlight* magazine. 'While so many other showbands take great pains to present a show, that, in its regimentation, would make a drilling sergeant proud, these seven men present a devil-may-care attitude that is so pleasing and refreshing, it is like a breath of spring air . . . . And that is what the business is all about. Give the fans something that is different and you are a hit. Too many bands are still scratching at the surface of this tough business.'

On a visit to The Arcadia, The Clipper Carlton gave The Capitol a huge plug for the following week, to such an extent that over 3,000 crowded in, something unheard of for a new band.

'We didn't go down well at all,' says Eamonn Monahan. 'We left Cork and did not go back for eight or nine months until we got the band right. When we went back we were able to draw in 4,000 fans on a Saturday night. The three bands who hold the record for the largest crowd in The Arcadia are The Capitol, The Royal and Jimmy Shand.'

Paddy Cole still recalls playing in The Crystal Ballroom in Dublin with the queue right around to South Anne Street and up Dawson Street, past the Mansion House.

'Paddy Kennedy, the famous Kerry footballer, was managing the ballroom for Bill Fuller, and it was hell for leather until the "House Full" sign went up,' says Cole. 'It was the same around the country. They'd use a shoe-horn to pack them in if they could. Tom Costello, who later managed Johnny McEvoy, and owns Westland Studios on Lombard St., also worked in the Crystal.'

There was very keen competition between the showbands as to who could draw the biggest crowd, even down to which band could close the doors the earliest. Eamonn Monahan recalls how Noel Finan who ran The Seapoint Ballroom in Galway, would offer his personal ratings:

'We would be on stage from 9p.m. to 1a.m. without a break. During the night we'd hear that the doors were closed at twenty minutes to nine, a total of 2,600 inside, and another thousand outside trying to get in. Noel would say: "You lads closed the doors at twenty to nine. The Royal closed them at half past eight last week".'

Despite the rivalry, the showbands were friendly with each other. A particular friendship existed between The Capitol and The Royal. That friendship helped guard against ballroom owners playing one off against the other.

'We had to watch promoters and try to synchronise ourselves with The Royal,' says Eamonn Monahan.

Bands had to guard themselves against their managements, too. Paddy Cole remembers The Capitol once discovering that Leo Keaney, who owned a ballroom in Letterkenny, could only book the band provided he also booked the Miami, which had just been launched, for three dates as well.

'Dickie Rock and The Miami were launched that way on the strength of The Capitol,' he says.

Soon other bands emerged around the country. The Cadets were the first showband to appear in military uniforms, and Eileen Reid topped hers off with a beehive hairdo that defied gravity. Thousands of young impressionable girls admired Reid's nasal singing of country songs about lost love. They gasped when she appeared on stage wearing a white wedding dress to plug her latest record.

From Mullingar came Joe Dolan and The Drifters, all dressed in red suits. Their first hit was Burt Bacharach's *The Answer to Everything* which catapulted them into the top league.

From Dublin came The Jim Farrelly Big Band. From Ballymena came The Freshmen, one of the most gifted bands to emerge in the country. Saxophonist Billy Brown arranged harmonies like nobody else, and the voices of the band blended together easily and naturally.

Meanwhile, Paddy Cole was enjoying his new found fame and the lifestyle that came with it.

'I had my first drink in the Country Club in Portmarnock in 1964. We were launching our first record and I drank a few bottles of Guinness. It was a wild night. One RTE producer, who had a few too many, climbed up a tree, and we spent a long time trying to coax him down. I was a late starter on the gargle, but I made up for it since!'

There was plenty of devilment, too. When in Dublin The Clipper Carlton stayed in Wynnes Hotel. Old Hugh Tourish used to insist that an old fashioned po be left in his room because of his weak kidneys.

'One night,' says Cole, 'some of the lads emptied a packet of Andrews liver salts into the po, so that when Tourish used it in the dark the place was awash with bubbles and fizz. Tourish became so alarmed about his condition he rang the doctor in the middle of the night!'

In their flat in Glasnevin Cole and Johnny Kelly were joined by roadie Gabriel Duffy, known affectionately as 'the Duff'.

'Dr Frank Dwane, a friend of mine, had given me a tonic, a side-effect of which was to turn your urine blue. One evening Johnny and I slipped some of it into the Duff's tea. So I started a conversation about a "new" deadly form of venereal disease known as "the blue piss" because of the change in the colour of the urine of those who contracted it. Johnny Kelly said thousands had already died from it. It was absolutely fatal for the poor unfortunates who caught it.

'The Duff listened with interest. The following morning Kelly and I came down for breakfast, but there was no sign of the Duff. Eventually I went up to his room.

"Get up Duff, it's half past ten," I shouted, but there was no response. He had hidden himself under the blankets. Eventually as I was going down the stairs, he whispered to me: "Pssst...Hey Paddy".

"What's wrong with you?" says I.

"I've got IT, Paddy!" he whispered shyly.

"You've got what, Duff?"

"The blue piss. I've got the blue piss!"

"It must have been that strange looking bird you were with the other night," I laughed, and walked off.

By now Paddy Cole had also bought his first car, a Volkswagen beetle.

'Eamonn Monahan came with to help me do the deal. The guy wanted £315 for it. Immediately Eamonn shouts out: "A bargain, done!" But being a dealing man from along the border, it broke my heart not to knock him down to £300. I still remember the number, ZX 4834."

That car was soon traded in for a new model as the money rolled in.

'Volkswagen beetles were really hip at the time. We had the double-bumpers and all the embellishments.'

Even car deals were kept within the music circle. Paddy bought his new car from Mick Quinn in Harold's Cross, who was later to go on to manage The Dubliners, Danny Doyle and The Pacific Showband.

But the young Cole did remember Phil Giblin's advice not to forget his family. Each week he sent £20 back to 'Blaney to help the family, and he bought a car for his father.

Things were looking up.

4

DOING AN ALBUM IN JUST THREE HOURS

In the summer of 1963 a shy, young man was playing the piano in the bar of the Great Northern Hotel in Bundoran, Co. Donegal. His playing caught the attention of Eamonn Monahan of The Capitol Showband, who was on holiday there. He approached the pianist, congratulated him on his playing, and asked him his name.

'Phil Coulter,' he replied.

'He was a nice, chatty fellow,' says Monahan. 'He was only 18 or 19 at the time, but it was the beginning of a long relationship.'

A few months later Coulter heard The Capitol were in The Allingham Hotel in Bundoran and went to see them.

After the gig, the late night session started and continued into the early hours. When Eamonn Monahan took a break from the piano, Coulter asked could he fill in.

'Fire away,' replied Monahan.

The budding songwriter seized the opportunity to play a number he had written called *Foolin' Time*. Butch Moore was impressed and asked for a copy.

The Royal Showband had already made a record, and The Capitol were under pressure to come up with an original. They chose *Foolin' Time.*

Coulter was another remarkable musician to emerge from Derry, which had already produced top names like The Quigleys and The McIntyres. *Foolin' Time* climbed to Number Three in the charts in 1964.

Coulter followed up with another single, *I Missed You*, but it failed to repeat the success. 'I thought it was a great record,' said Coulter. 'I still think it's a great record. Paddy Cole did a fine baritone sax on it.'

Working with The Capitol brought Phil Coulter to the attention of Phil Solomon, who promoted the band in Britain. This opened up new opportunities to work with other bands and artists including The Bachelors, Van Morrison and Sandy Shaw (Coulter wrote her Eurovision hit *Puppet on a String*).

Coulter maintained close links with The Capitol and among other projects, made a record with them called *Born to be With You*, which had been a hit for The Cordettes in the 1950s.

Meanwhile, in 1962 and a year on the road as a full showband professional, trumpeter Paul Sweeney decided to leave and return to his architectural studies. Sweeney was replaced by a Cork man, Bram McCarthy, who had played with another great band, The Mick Delahunty Orchestra. McCarthy was a great reader of music and a top-class Dixieland musician.

Life was hectic for the members of The Capitol. Apart from the nightly gigs across the country, they had their own weekly programme on Radio Luxembourg, which began in October 1963. This meant getting up early on Monday mornings to be in the Tommy Ellis Studios on Mount Street by 10a.m. Ellis recorded the tunes, edited the programme and sent it off to Radio Luxembourg for transmission.

Each Wednesday at 7.45p.m. the familiar sound of The Capitol reached thousands of listeners throughout Britain and Ireland. Letters poured in from all over Ireland, England, Scotland and Wales at the rate of 500 per day until the series ended. To deal with the mail The Capitol Fan Club was set up at 67 Cabra Road in Phibsboro, run by Monica McNelis and Maire Hurley.

While the Royal was the first showband to record a single, The Capitol was the first with an album. *The Many Faces of The Capitol* was made under the direction of Fred O'Donovan in the Eamon Andrews studios by a London recording company, Delyse.

The general manager of Delyse was Isabella Wallich, niece of the co-founder of the gramophone industry, Fred Gaisbert. With Emile Berliner, inventor of the gramophone, she laid the foundations of the industry. In 1955, with a staff of three, Isabella Wallich made her first record. Her aim was to 'produce fine gramophone records with first-class artistes, worthwhile material and the best that recording techniques can achieve'. The fact that The Capitol were selected by Delyse as their first recording in Ireland was a striking compliment to the eight Irish musicians.

'We set up the microphones just like on a stage and recorded the whole album in three hours,' says Paddy. 'We were pioneering figures. These days bands take a whole year off to do one album.'

The album contained numbers which had lilted their way into the hearts of thousands of fans — *Angelina, You' ll never Walk Alone, My Lovely Irish Rose* and *Silver Threads and Golden Needles.*

In the ballrooms The Capitol put on ever more sophisticated performances, employing writers like Cecil Sheridan to provide material for their shows.

The full performance lasted five hours. The Capitol opened with an hour of Dixieland music featuring Don Long on trombone, Paul Sweeney (later Bram McCarthy) on trumpet and Paddy Cole on clarinet.

Then four guys would take a break and the other three continue. When Johnny Kelly took a break, or moved up front to sing a few country numbers, Paddy Cole took over as drummer. There was a good mix of country and western music featuring Des Kelly and his brother, Johnny. A major attraction during their nightly shows was *The Parade of the Showbands* during which they took off other showbands.

'For 20 minutes the crowd would stop dancing and gather around the front of the stage — 15 or 20 rows deep — to watch us pay tribute to the other bands.'

By the end of the night everyone was exhausted, mainly as a result of the inadequate ventilation and the huge crowds.

'Your suit would be soaked,' says Cole. 'That's mainly the reason I have rheumatism today. There were no shower facilities or anything like that. You just towelled yourself as best you could.'

Road manager Sean Jordan spotted the problem. He bought track suits and put the musicians through their paces to make them fit. In the dressing room after dances he towelled the musicians individually and applied liberal amounts of talcum powder.

'The halls were so packed that there was a saying going around at the time: "I haven't seen the floorboards in six months".'

The showband industry created a huge spin-off for the economy. Hairdressing salons mushroomed all over the country, the rag trade got a boost, and there was a bonanza for pubs, restaurants, and filling stations all over the country. Every showband needed transport. They also needed instruments, many changes of clothing and sound equipment. A huge business was created in publicity, advertising and printing. There was even talk among some members of The Capitol of running their own dances.

'The idea was brought up one night in the wagon on the way back from Lalor's Hotel in Naas, a regular venue for the band. The disagreement nearly led to the break-up of The Capitol. Paul Sweeney wanted The Capitol to get into buying property, but others were totally opposed, saying our job was solely to play music.'

When it came to publicity for the showbands, the most important publication was *Spotlight* magazine.

Founded by Murt Lucey of Cork and local journalist John Coughlan, it was the bible for all those involved in the showband industry. A front cover photograph of a particular showband on *Spotlight* guaranteed a boost in sales and increased bookings.

'But,' claims Cole, 'if you didn't take ads in the magazine, then you didn't get the write-ups. If you were featured on the front cover, you had to take so many ads. Eventually you had to pay for the cover. It was all hype.'

An ongoing row between The Capitol and the management of *Spotlight* meant the band got no coverage for a long period. But one of the journalists, Michael Hand, later editor of the *Sunday Independent* approached Cole to write a piece about him.

'Michael wrote an article about me fishing on the Dodder and that healed the rift. I could see both sides. They had a magazine to run, we were in the showband business. John Coughlan, the editor was a stubborn little man, but Hand healed the rift.'

In addition to *Spotlight*, the *New Musical Gazette* was published in Longford by Jimmy Molloy and supported financially by Albert Reynolds. Its contributors included Fr Brian D'Arcy, former *Sunday World* editor Colm McClelland and *Irish Independent* columnist Sam Smyth, who had managed ballrooms in Belfast.

The growth in ballrooms meant that owners and proprietors could entice overseas artists and guarantee them nationwide tours. Artists who toured Ireland in the early '60s included Kenny Ball, Hank Locklin, Chubby Checker, Johnny Cash, Jim Reeves, Adam Faith and Little Richard.

Such was the effect of the music industry on the economy that in 1965 Butch Moore declared: 'It's about time this country, from the Government down, began to realise that the biggest industry in Ireland at the moment is showbands.'

The band developed a huge army of regular fans who followed The Capitol wherever they played.

'We would see the same women tonight in the Olympic Ballroom, tomorrow night in Portmarnock, and the following night in Bray. There were five or six guys from Belfast who followed us everywhere. Of course, they were also chasing the women who followed The Capitol. I remember these guys driving down to Dundalk, and even as far south as Waterford — Leslie, Andy, Dominic, Alfie and Jackie. They drove unbelievable journeys in the middle of the week. I don't know how they stuck it. All the bands had fans like these.'

Not everyone was a fan of The Capitol, of course, and sometimes there were encounters with the fans of rival bands, most notably The Royal.

'There was a loyal band of Royal fans in Dundalk, and when they saw our wagon they would follow us and make rude signs.'

The Capitol fans were no saints either. The fan club once organised a train to bring supporters from Dublin to a dance in Carlow town. The plan was to walk from the station to the ballroom. However, *en route* they diverted to go past the home of TJ Byrne, manger of The Royal. There they stopped and chanted outside.

'We knew nothing about it, and thought it was a dreadful thing to do when we heard about it later,' says Cole.

Like today's soccer teams, each band had its own solid following — Johnny Quigley in Derry, Johnny Flynn in Tuam and so on.

Within months of turning professional, The Capitol became so popular they were regularly called 'The Fabulous Capitol', 'The Incomparable Capitol', 'Ireland's Greatest Attraction', and 'The Glamour Boys of the Dancing World'.

'In 1961 people didn't come to dance,' said Des Kelly. 'They shouted and screamed and tried to pull you off the stage . . . . We were all completely knocked out at the reception we got all over the country. I doubt very much if some of the scenes will ever be repeated in Ireland. '

The Capitol were as popular in the North as south of the Border. The music united Protestant and Catholic, unionist and nationalist.

'We loved going up to the North, and had wonderful times there. We always managed to play a bit of golf in Portrush or Portstewart.'

Sammy Barr was a character who owned The Flamingo Ballroom in Ballymena. An entrepreneur in his own right, he had pioneered the 'hot dog' before most others spotted the potential. Barr had once bought up thousands of prams, believing there would be a huge demand for the particular make. When the demand did not materialise, he went to his local bank manager, former rugby international Willie John MacBride, for advice.

'Sammy,' said MacBride, 'what you should now do is go around the country and buy up all the condoms you can get from every chemist's shop. In nine months time there will be a huge run on your prams!'

'Dermot O'Brien went up there and sang the *Merry Ploughboy* in Barr's Hall,' says Cole. 'But when he did, there was a minor riot among the mixed crowd. When Sammy used to say to you: "There's a very mixed crowd here tonight", what he really meant was: "The whole crowd is Protestant but the band is Catholic".

'About a week after the riot over Dermot O'Brien's song, we arrived and heard Sammy had been upset by the hassle and had gone home early the previous week. So we decided to play a trick on him.

"Hey, Sammy," we said. "We've got a real show-stopper tonight."

"Ah, great," replied Sammy, "I love a show-stopper. What's it called?"

'And we all began in chorus: "In Mountjoy jail one Monday morning . . . ."

"Ahm . . . I'll be seeing ye boys," said Sammy, as he made a hasty exit by the back door.'

Eamonn Monahan was equally struck by the relative lack of any hostility to bands from the Republic.

'I often saw eight or ten RUC men singing *The Old Orange Flute* in Ballymena, and we would sing *Sean South*. There was no animosity whatsoever. Of course, that all changed in 1969.'

But there was often tension over whether to play the British or Irish National Anthem at the end of a dance.

Royal pianist Gerry Cullen remembers a particular incident in one ballroom in the North when two RAF men pulled Tom Dunphy from the stage because he refused to play the British

National Anthem. Dunphy pointed out that the instructions from the management were to play neither.

Before the band left for home, the military police brought the RAF men out to The Royal wagon and made them apologise for their behaviour.

Success for The Capitol led to trips abroad. The band toured England, striking the right note with the public.

'Our agent in London, Phil Solomon, tried to create the image that none of us was supposed to have girlfriends or be married. The idea was that girls might say they had a chance with such and such a fellow. But everybody at home knew what the real situation was.'

Their first tour of the United States came during the six weeks of Lent in 1961, when the ballrooms at home practically shut down. The trip was arranged by Bill Fuller, the highly successful Kerry man, who owned The Crystal Ballroom in Dublin and had a string of ballrooms in the States, in the cities of New York, Boston, Chicago and Philadelphia. In New York The Capitol adopted a new local, The Old Stand bar, owned by Pat and Margo Corr from Cavan.

'Being a country band that came from areas of high emigration — two from Donegal, two from Galway, Paddy came from Monaghan, Don and Bram from Cork — we drew big crowds in the States,' says Eamonn Monahan. 'The Royal and ourselves could draw anything up to 3,500 people in New York, which at $5 each was not bad in 1961.'

Bill Fuller practically controlled dancing in America. Apart from his own ballrooms, he would sell the band on to other promoters right up to Toronto. 'We were grossing £8,000 to £10,000 a week in today's money, but we had no sense. We thought everyone else was earning the same.'

Bands made — and spent — a lot of money, much of it foolishly.

'It was an age when you felt you had to look well, even on a night off,' says Cole. 'You were still on stage and people would look at you and judge you on how you were dressed. A lot of fellows thought it would never end. We stayed in the best hotels and had the best of everything. And, of course, we all wore sheepskin coats, the status symbol of the age. And we were right! This was to signify that you were on the crest of a wave.

'I remember once we took over the wing of The Cumberland Hotel in London. Journalists, hangers-on, the lot, all booked in — and we paying the lot, flights and all. The residents' bar ran out of drink during the night.'

Drink led to the downfall of many stars. Several musicians were very heavy drinkers. Some became alcoholics.

'It was a terrible temptation at all times,' says Cole. 'Once we were flying to America and were only an hour out of Dublin when the bar was out of drink because of the band and all the people travelling with us.

'As well as that, ballroom owners were so delighted to be getting such big crowds that they would leave a few crates of beer and a couple of bottles of whiskey in the dressing rooms. After the dance the session would start. Some of these drinking sessions were unbelievable.

'Many musicians needed a drink before they went on stage. Either they were shy, or they didn't fully believe in what they were doing. A lot of them ended up as alcoholics. I remember comedian Noel Ginnity saying to me, after he had sold a pub in Drogheda: "Why do we have to wait until we are down in the gutter before we pull ourselves back up again?"

'You thought drinking was the thing to do because everyone else did it. On Monday night, which was our free night, we would go down to The Television Club, and the drinking sessions were fierce there, too.'

When Cole first came to Dublin, Paddy McNally, an old school pal, introduced him to The Old Stand pub on Dublin's Exchequer St., where the manager, Louis Dignam was a native of Ballybay. Dignam was a good friend of the actor Yul Brunner, who used to send round a taxi to bring him to The Gresham Hotel for dinner.

'Everybody, from sports stars to entertainers, congregated in The Old Stand because of Louis. When Louis took a break at 10p.m. for fifteen minutes and went across the street to The International for a drink, the pub emptied as everyone followed him across.

'Among the regulars were Dublin footballers Tony Hanahoe and Jimmy Keaveny, as well as Kevin Beahan, who had won an All-Ireland with Louth, surgeon Matt McHugh, who played in goal for Cavan and Martin McArdle, a Monaghan man who worked for Superquinn. Dignam always referred to players who had come in to the bar by their number on the Dublin team, never by their name. So he told you: "Number 11 is on the other side."

'It was a very sad occasion for all of us when Louis died. Eamonn Monahan and myself played in the church at his funeral. I remember during the ceremony Tony Hanahoe whispered to me: "Isn't it a great tribute to the little man's integrity that he died a barman." The common perception was that the barman ended up owning the bar.

'We also frequented Dermot Sheehan's pub on nearby Chatam Street where there was a great music tradition. There I used to meet trombonist Jack Bayle (currently with the Paddy Cole band), Joe McIntyre from Derry, and Benny McNeil, the trumpet player with the RTE Concert Orchestra, John Curran, and Earl Gill.

'One night Paddy McNally came into The Television Club and I was drinking a naggin of neat whiskey. I offered him a drop.

"Have you no mixer?" he asked.

"Not at all, Paddy, you don't need a mixer for that. It's only a drop of whiskey," I replied.

McNally stared at me with disbelief and warned me that I was "mad in the head" to be drinking neat whiskey. It was a timely warning for me and just as well for me that I took heed of McNally.'

Another man to teach Paddy Cole a lesson about drinking was Albert Reynolds.

'We were to play a date in Muff, Co. Donegal, but it was cancelled because there had been a bad accident and five members of a Derry band were killed. We drove back to Dublin again, but stopped off in The Longford Arms Hotel, then owned by the Reynolds brothers, Albert and Jim.

'At the time I used to drink the odd bottle of stout only. So I ordered a bottle for myself. However, Charlie McBrien, a non-drinker and manager of the Mighty Avons, was already in the bar and ordered brandy for everybody. So I had both. I was knocking back the stuff like sweet milk when Albert came over to me, looking surprised.

"I didn't know you drank shorts," he remarked.

"It's great stuff Albert," I said.

"Well, OK," said Albert, calling for another large brandy for me.

The last thing I remember is walking out the door of the hotel. Whoever was walking behind me caught me falling. I was never as sick in my life. When I got back to Dublin, I called up to Helen, who I was going out with at the time and was to be my future wife. She shared a flat with two other girls, Phena O'Boyle and Ailish McGavigan. I rang the doorbell around midnight, but they were afraid to answer.

"Who is it?" they shouted out from inside.

But I found that I couldn't speak. All that would come out was: "Aw . . . aw . . . aw . . . hic!"

Eventually they opened the door and one of them gasped: "My God, Helen, he's GREEN." I couldn't speak a single word. The girls gave me cups of coffee and eventually I came round. I finished up driving around the city in my VW with all the windows open, trying to get a breath of fresh air. I reckon Albert did that just to teach me a lesson, the best lesson I ever got. To this day, if anyone gives me a brandy I can still remember the sickness when I smell it. I must have sounded very cocky in myself for Albert to do that to me.'

In later years as Minister and Taoiseach, Albert Reynolds was a good friend to Paddy Cole.

'I watched his political career with interest and pride. As soon as he became Taoiseach and leader of Fianna Fáil, I got a call to play at the Árdfheis twice. I also played at his daughter Miriam's wedding in Kilmainham. Whenever he sees me at a function he comes up for a chat, or he'll pass a remark in public like: "We're going to have a good night, I see Cole and the boys are here." He has always remembered the boys in the business. He was a hard worker himself, and we in the business are all proud of him.'

Some of the hotels suffered from the excesses of the band members, and they got a bad name. The Dixies were notorious for fun-making. 'You'd ring up a hotel and the receptionist would say: "No, the Dixies were here last week, we're not taking any more bands." The Dixies left a trail of destruction all over Ireland, but all the bands loved them. They got up to every devilment.'

On tours of England, they would hire a limousine and drive from London to Birmingham with crates of beer on the floor. The two characters of the band were Joe Mac and the bass guitarist, Christy O'Mahony.

On one such trip, Christy, winking at the lads, looked at the driver and declared loudly: 'I think that fellow was with the Black and Tans.'

'Don't be ridiculous, Christy, he was not,' said Joe Mac.

'He was, I've seen his face before, he was with the Tans for sure.'

'No, Christy, he was not, definitely NOT.'

But Christy was not for persuading. He sprang from the back seat and lunged at the hapless driver.

The quick-thinking driver pulled in, locked the entire band in the car and phoned the police from a call-box. They arrived and arrested The Dixies. The joke had backfired badly.

Other times O'Mahony would pretend he was blind. In West Cork, Joe Mac led him into a public house and set him up at the counter. 'Don't pass any remarks about this blind fucker here!', Mac said to the barman.

The barman warned Mac about his language. When a drink was ready, the barman set it in front of O'Mahony, and carefully put his hands around it. However, the 'blind' O'Mahony immediately spilled it.

'You blind bastard!' roared Mac from the corner.

This time the barman ordered Mac to leave the premises for insulting the 'handicapped' customer. With that the 'blind' O'Mahony felt his way over to the dart board and hit three perfect targets. Both Mac and O'Mahony ran out the back door, pursued by a very angry barman, warning them never to come near the premises again.

The Capitol, too, had their lighter moments. Johnny Kelly, the drummer, was a little nervous of flying and always had a drink or two before taking off. The band flew to Birmingham to play at a function organised by Irish promoter Frank McCloone. Taxis were organised to pick them up at the airport. Cole and Kelly shared one.

'Where to, Paddy?' demanded the driver in a typically derogatory manner.

'Don't you call him "Paddy",' roared a high-spirited Kelly.

Cole rushed to hold back his colleague from attacking the driver.

'I'm very sorry, sir,' said the driver, 'but in the pub I drink in, there are lots of Irish customers, and we call them all "Paddy". I didn't mean any offence.'

'That's OK,' replied Cole, who had finally managed to calm down Kelly.

'Anyway, what is your name, sir?' asked the driver.

'Err . . . er . . . er . . . Paddy,' muttered an embarrassed Cole!

In Ballymena, The Capitol happened upon an automatic photo machine in Sammy Barr's Flamingo Ballroom.

'We had never seen this type of machine before,' says Eamonn Monahan, 'so we examined it closely. We decided to try it out and searched our pockets for half-a-crown. Johnny Kelly went off to a shop for one, but in the meantime Butch Moore arrived with a half-crown and went into the machine. He pulled down his trousers and exposed his bottom to the the camera. Johnny Kelly duly arrived back, put in his half-crown, went in and smiled for the camera. Minutes later Johnny's face was aghast when four rather obscene snaps dropped into the tray!'

Much of the drinking and arguing arose from boredom. Musicians were away for home for up to six days a week, living close to each other, travelling, eating, rehearsing and performing together. It was a recipe for disaster. So, too, was the mixing of wives.

'Musicians used to bring their wives to gigs everywhere and it was a pain in the arse for everyone,' says Cole. 'You couldn't change because they were in the dressing room. When you came off stage they were there sitting in front of you.'

Rows erupted on tours abroad.

'Once we were in Toronto, waiting to go to the airport. The row started between Eamonn Monahan and Johnny Kelly. Johnny kept teasing Eamonn shouting at him: "Hit me, hit me". Suddenly Eamonn hit him and the fisticuffs started. I just grabbed the two of them by the scruff of the neck and threw them out of my bedroom. Johnny had been smoking a cigarette at the time and sparks flew everywhere.'

After the excitement Cole lay down on the bed for a rest. Suddenly the mattress was in flames.

'I got some water and quenched it, but to be sure I rang reception to tell them. Five minutes later five or six burly firemen arrived like a herd of elephants and took the door off the hinges with axes. They poured water on everything and wrecked the room.

'I was standing in the foyer when I heard the manger enquire for "Mr Cole in connection with the fire bill". I slipped out quietly and took a taxi directly to the airport.'

'We simply got on each other's nerves. It was the same with all the bands. Some of the rows in The Capitol were unbelievable. Mostly they were drink related. It was something other groups learned to avoid later on, by travelling separately to functions and not seeing each other too often.

'In the band these days we are more mature. We don't do things that annoy others. We try to confine our arguments to how to make the show better. These days, if I fly off the handle, I suddenly notice there's nobody listening. They all disperse and I have the argument all to myself.'

Dublin solicitor Eddie Masterson, a popular personality among the showband fraternity, provided a shoulder to cry on for many musicians. A native of Sligo, he first practised in Carrickmacross before moving to Dublin. A man with a keen interest in music himself — he composed *Lovely Leitrim* for Larry Cunningham and wrote *A Tribute to Jim Reeves* — he regularly poured oil on troubled waters between musicians and management, and between musicians themselves.

Eddie lived in Barry's Hotel and was a practical joker. He once left word for Micky O'Neill, the drummer with the Big 8, to be in the Garden of Remembrance in blazer and pants, and drumsticks in hand, at 9.30a.m. for a photocall. The message was allegedly left by the band's manager, TJ Byrne. The following morning Masterson passed by the Garden of Remembrance, on his way to work, and saw O'Neill standing inside, looking foolish, and dressed in an immaculate blue jacket and white pants. Masterson beamed.

'Hey, Micky, have a nice day!', he roared at the hapless drummer.

Paddy Cole has fond memories of Eddie Masterson.

'You always felt better when you talked to Eddie. He was one of the most popular of men.'

There was fun on the road, too. Catching out their road manager, Sean 'The Spoofer' Jordan, was part of the fun.

'There was a guard from Ballybay, Brian McCarthy, who was stationed in Kilcock. He would regularly come to our gigs in and around Dublin. Once, when we were going to The Traveller's

Friend in Castlebar, we arranged for Brian to stop the wagon, unknown to the Spoofer.'

The Capitol set out from Dublin with the Spoofer, as always, driving and speaking in the 'ben lang' dialect, frequently used by showbands. Outside Kilcock a uniformed garda emerged from the side of the road and flagged them down.

'What is this "berkeley hunt" looking for?' muttered an anxious Spoofer.

'Yes guard, what's the problem?' he asked impatiently.

'You've been speeding,' said the guard abruptly.

'No, I couldn't be, there's a governor on this engine,' said the Spoofer. Turning over his shoulder to the band members, he muttered: 'I'll have this fellow herding sheep in Kerry by the middle of next week.'

'Who are you any way, a football team?' asked the guard.

'No, we are NOT a football team. We are The Capitol Showband,' said a proud Spoofer.

'I'm afraid sir, you'll have to get out and walk the white line,' said the guard authoritatively.

At this point Paddy Cole leaned forward and urged the Spoofer to tell the guard to get lost.

'No,' replied the Spoofer, 'the easiest thing is to co-operate. I can walk the white line, no problem.'

Cole ignored the Spoofer and leaned out the window:

'Listen here, guard, we don't have to listen here to this shit. Fuck off with yourself. Drive on, Spoofer.'

Guard McCarthy burst out laughing and an angry Spoofer was not impressed.

Six weeks later The Capitol Showband was passing through nearby Maynooth. Suddenly a garda patrol flagged down the driver, Spoofer Jordan. Without thinking the Spoofer opened the window.

'Guard, you can fuck off . . . and tell your friend McCarthy to fuck off as well. We're in a hurry to a gig.'

'Excuse me,' snapped the guard. 'Pull in and get out of that van at once!'

It took frantic telephone calls, and endless explanations from the band members to save Spoofer from being arrested.

Meanwhile, a fire which had wrecked his flat on Botanic Road, had forced Paddy Cole to Ranelagh.

'When we went on tour to the United States, we left the flat to promoter Noel Carthy, and his brother Brendan, who fell asleep with a cigarette, and the place went up in flames. When we came home, all we saw were the charred remains of radiograms, suits and records. Of course we had no insurance.

'We moved into a house on Oakley Road, Ranelagh, owned by a Mr and Mrs Armstrong. They were very kind to us. If they heard us coming in late, they would give us a reminder to look after ourselves.

In Ranelagh Paddy Cole lived close to the McIntyres from Derry and Tony Woods, who played with The Rhythm Boys.

'Everything revolved around music. We used to listen to songs like Frank Sinatra singing *Old Man River*, count the number of bars between breaths and have heated discussions about it. Then we would head up for a few pints in Russell's pub, where the discussion would start again.'

Paddy Cole later lost touch with the Armstrongs. Then, one night during a reunion of The Capitol in the Braemor Rooms in 1984, he discovered a request from them in a left-over bundle of notes when the show had finished. 'I was disappointed that I never saw it until the show was over. They must have thought: "Your man Cole forgot us very fast". Unfortunately, they had moved out of their home in Ranelagh, and I could not contact them. I would still love to meet them.'

5

A FOX IN BUTCH MOORE'S BED

One hot sunny afternoon in New York in the early 1960s a group of Irish musicians could be seen hauling a load of instruments and amplifiers along Fifth Avenue. American promoter Bill Fuller had hired a studio for The Capitol Showband to make some recordings, and the musicians had underestimated the distance. They were accompanied by Joe Ruane, Bill Fuller's right-hand man.

'We were told the studio was one block away from our hotel, but discovered it was eight,' says Cole.

Eventually they arrived at the studio, dishevelled and teeming with sweat. The musicians set up their equipment.

While Butch Moore was in the dressing room, feeling a little depressed and under stress, Paddy Cole slipped into the studio, grabbed a black crayon and wrote on the wall: 'Elvis Presley, hope I make it'.

Butch Moore duly arrived out and went into the studio to record. When he had finished, he came out and began telling his colleagues that the sound engineer had said that Presley had recorded in the studio some time before. Elvis had, in fact, autographed the wall of the studio, Moore claimed.

'Would you shut up, you bloody eejit,' laughed Eamonn Monahan, 'It was Paddy Cole wrote that.'

Moore did not speak to Monahan for a month, even though it was Cole who had set him up.

The band recorded two numbers, *My Lagan Love* and *If You Want To Be Happy*, but Bill Fuller refused to pay the duty on the records when they arrived in Dublin Airport. Consequently they were never released in Ireland.

While in New York, the band regularly stayed at The Woodward Hotel, affectionately known in showbusiness as the 'The Woodworm'. The hotel was close to The City Center Ballroom, which saw thousands of American–Irish fans come to hear The Clipper Carlton, The Capitol, The Royal and many other showbands.

All the musicians were looked after by Arthur, the friendly night porter, who took special care of them.

'Arthur was a lovely man,' says Cole. 'He was into Gospel music and religion. He used to say to me: "Paddy, in this country we've got yellow men, black men, white men and red men, but we don't have any of those orange men you've got over there in Ireland".

Eamonn Monahan, a prankster, once sent a naive Butch Moore to ask Arthur to tell the traffic policeman outside the hotel to stop blowing his whistle for two hours because the band needed to get some sleep.

'On another occasion, Tommy O'Brien, who had been a famous band leader in Dublin and was then band leader in Fuller's New State Ballroom in Boston, drove us out to New Haven to a gig. We packed the gear up on the roof rack and took off. However, out on the highway, Butch Moore's guitar fell off on to the road, and a truck drove over it. You can imagine the state of it, with the neck broken. Very late in the night we arrived back to the Woodward, with a sad-looking Butch still carrying the broken guitar.

'Arthur, as usual, let us in.

"Rough gig tonight guys?" he quipped, spotting the guitar. "They're a tough crowd out in New Haven!"

While some of the dances were rough, when the fighting started, the members of The Capitol made their excuses and left. For Paddy Cole, his lips were his livelihood, and he protected them at all cost.

'There was a special farewell in the Woodward for the bouncers who worked for Bill Fuller in New York. A difference of opinion erupted between some of them, and there was the mother of all rows. I dived under a table for cover only to find Don Long, the trombonist, there before me. We had to protect our lips because they were our bread and butter. One slap and you were out of work. The fighting was just the norm for them, but it frightened the life out of us.'

Paddy Cole had thought Glasgow tough. Soon he discovered that England, like New York, could be worse. The Casey brothers from Kerry ran a chain of ballrooms in England. They were strong men, trained in wrestling.

'You had to have tough men running these ballrooms because there were some very tough guys around at that time. There were regular fisticuffs in all these places. One of the most vicious rows I ever witnessed was in the Irish Hall in New Cross in London.

'Twelve or fourteen English miners came in and, against the rules, brought drink down on to the dance floor. When one of the bouncers reprimanded them, they made a derogatory reference to his Irishness and told him "to fuck off". With that all the bouncers arrived and a most vicious fight followed. The bouncers got the better of the miners and beat them senseless. Like the saloon piano player in the Western movies when the shooting starts, we had to keep going, even though there was no one on the floor except these guys slogging it out.'

But the show went on, and so did the dreaded rehearsals.

'We regularly rehearsed in Desmond Domican's dance studio in Parnell Square, but more usually in the halls around the country. If we played in Killarney tonight, we would get up early tomorrow morning and rehearse, or else move on to the next stop and rehearse there. It was not conducive to having a happy time. Often we were too tired and tempers would fray.'

Rehearsals went on for a couple of hours at a time. As the band could not have music on stage, they memorised each number. They would listen to the chart hits of the day. The rhythm sections would get the chords down, while Butch wrote down the lyrics. The Capitol even got a special record-player fitted in the wagon so that they could learn tunes as they drove up and down the country.

'I remember rehearsal sessions in the Strandhill in Sligo while the sun was splitting the rocks outside. I used to loathe them. We should have been out playing a round of golf. The relaxation would have been far more beneficial.'

All the time the popularity of The Capitol continued to soar. In the Spring of 1964, they were invited to appear at The London Palladium. Roy Orbison topped the bill, and the other guests included The Bachelors and The Big Four. The Capitol band went down a treat with the live audience and got a standing ovation.

The Palladium brought further offers from Britain, but The Capitol declined them, preferring to concentrate on the home scene. The end of '64 saw further hits for the band, including *Down Came the Rain* and *Born To Be With You*, which was arranged by Phil Coulter.

But the greatest triumph came with an appearance on *Sunday Night at The Palladium* on 24 January 1965.

'It was the pinnacle in anyone's career,' says Cole. 'It was not big over here because television was in its infancy, but it had an audience of 30 million viewers.'

'The Capitol Showband prepares for the greatest thrill of their career — tomorrow night's Palladium Show — and they intend to present their full repertoire,' wrote dancing correspondent Paul Jones in the *Evening Press* on the eve of the performance. 'Butch Moore is recognised, even in England, America and on the Continent of Europe as one of the greatest artists in the game, so much so that Sammy Davis Junior, who heard his *Foolin' Time* while on a British tour, said: "Who is this guy Moore? I'd like to meet him."'

As the band rehearsed their numbers, they looked down into the orchestral pit and saw top musicians like trombonist Don Lusher and trumpeter Kenny Baker.

'These were the guys whose records we used to collect. Bram McCarthy was overcome with nerves and fluffed a few notes on the trumpet. Kenny Baker spotted the problem, and came round to the dressing room.

"Listen here guys," he said, "what you are doing up there we couldn't do. We couldn't walk on and play without music". Then he had a chat with Bram about his trumpet and the whole situation relaxed. It was a nice gesture.'

On the night the show was to be broadcast, the former British Prime Minister, Winston Churchill, died and the show was recorded for later.

'I don't know if it was the fact that we were playing at The Palladium that finally pushed Churchill over the top or not, but the transmission was postponed for a week. The next Sunday we were playing in Wexford and watched a very snowy version on a TV screen there. We performed a number of tunes including, *Granada*, *Born to be With You* and *Down Came the Rain*.' In their rendition of Tommy Makem's *The Bould O'Donoghue*, the band neatly substituted Queen Elizabeth for Queen Victoria!

The following day the band gathered at the IBC studios in Portland Place to cut their latest disc. Former trumpeter Paul Sweeney flew over specially to join them.

Success at The Palladium saw even more offers pour in for the band. The Capitol were offered a six-month residency in The Palladium, but turned it down. 'Some of the guys were married and did not want to live in London. The offer was even worked in such a way out that we would fly home every Saturday night and have Sunday off. The move would have made us a real hit in England, but we didn't do it.'

The band also turned down major opportunities in the United States.

'We worked for a Monaghan man, Jimmy Barker, who was a first class promoter in New York. When we arrived at the airport there were limousines waiting for us and when we got to the ballroom, the equipment was there ready on stage. He was totally professional. He had a lot of influence in Villanova University, and we even learned their song: "V for Villanova, V for Victory. . . ."

'Jimmy had a coast-to-coast tour lined up for us, but we turned it down. He did it later for The Irish Rovers, who had a Number One hit with *The Unicorn*, and they now have their own TV series in Canada and are very wealthy as a result. We turned all that, and much more, down.'

'The Royal had already gone to Vegas and finished up being a bigger attraction than Fats Domino. They persevered, but we did not have that push. We would have tried to be too slick.'

Decisions on the band's future were made, mainly, by manager, Jim Doherty, and the band leader, Des Kelly. However, everybody was consulted on important issues.

'Really the band should not have been consulted at all because it used to end up a right free-for-all. I wanted to take up the Jimmy Barker offer because he had explained the potential to me, and he was no bullshitter.'

In 1965 RTE decided to take part in The Eurovision Song Contest for the first time. The station invited composers to send in their songs. A Kildare woman, Theresa Conlon, penned a song called *Walking the Streets in the Rain* and sent it off to RTE. There producer Tom McGrath selected the singers, and chose Butch Moore for the song.

It was the high point in Moore's career, to represent Ireland in Eurovision for the first time, in Naples. A long way from The Blue Clavons and The Ritz Ballroom in Ballyfermot.

Moore, as The Capitols' vocalist, was by far the best known of the band, and drew huge crowds. While he always looked cool, his appearance often betrayed an inner nervousness, which even extended to spiders and mice. He was frequently the victim of pranks by other members of The Capitol.

'One night,' Cole recalls, 'we were all staying in O'Meara's Hotel in Nenagh. It was a beautiful old world hotel with stuffed pheasants and a fox on the landing. We had a good few drinks there and before going to bed a few of us grabbed the stuffed fox and took it up to Butch's bedroom. There we put it under the sheets with just the head looking out. It was very realistic.

'We said "goodnight" to Butch, but immediately tip-toed back to his door. Through the keyhole we could see him singing and laughing to himself. The next thing we heard this unmerciful scream, and he nearly took the door off the hinges as he ran out screaming: "There's a dog in the room. . . . There's a dog in the room. . . ."'

The band travelled to Donegal. There they stayed in an old country house owned by Sean and Noreen Thomas, and situated between Donegal Town and Mount Charles, the home of Eamonn Monahan.

'Eamonn spent the evening telling Butch that the house was haunted while we were having a few drinks in Donegal. By the time we got back to the house, Butch was very nervous. The scene was set. I was sharing a room with him. We got into our beds. As I was dropping off to sleep Butch called me.

"Paddy?"

"Yea, what do you want?"

"Do you see that changing-screen over there?

"Yea, What about it?"

"Did you check to see if there was anything behind it?"

"For Christ's sake, Butch, would you go to sleep!"

Butch would not be silenced.

'In the end, for the sake of peace, I got up, folded the screen and went back to bed. I tried to fall asleep.

'But the next thing I heard:

"Paddy?"

"YES, What do you want NOW?"

"Do you want to go to the toilet?"

"NO, I do NOT."

"You should go, otherwise you'll have to get up during the night."

"Do YOU want to go, Butch?"

"Yes."

'He was afraid to go on his own because the toilet was at the other end of the corridor. The trees were blowing in the wind and it was very realistic.

'"For Christ's sake, Butch," said Cole, "I thought I was away from home and bringing the kids to the toilet. Get up fast and come on."

'We walked up the corridor, both of us in our underpants. He went in but as he was going to the toilet he kept the door open and was looking out at me. Suddenly I put on a terrible face as if I had seen something really frightening and ran off screaming: "Aaaaaaaaaarrgh!"

'The next thing was Butch came flying down the corridor, spraying both sides as he went!

'I told him that this was all a set-up by Eamonn Monahan. He went to bed happily. We were only in bed a few minutes when outside the window we heard a ghostly sound:

"AOOOO OOOOOO!"

'But this time the now brave Butch jumped out of the bed, opened the window and shouted into the darkness: "Go home, Monahan, you fuckin' eejit".'

On Saturday 20 March, 1965 Butch Moore was facing a more formidable test. And this one was for real.

Band Manager Jim Doherty, together with Des Kelly accompanied Butch to Naples where they rehearsed for a week beforehand. On the night of the show Butch's father, Tommy, who worked as a Dáil usher, appeared on the *Late Late Show*.

Butch's performance went perfectly. He was delighted to come sixth. Back in the dressing room he relaxed with a large brandy.

Back in Dublin, Moore was greeted by a large media horde who wanted to know, not about his Eurovision experience, but if he was married. Wives or girlfriends were never photographed with the band, and so the news that he had married in 1963, and now had three children, came as a shock to many.

The success in Naples brought more bookings and yet more fame for The Capitol. However, there were still difficulties with the British market.

'I remember being in a record shop in Camden Town,' says Cole, 'where the Irish girls were told not to stock the record because the powers-that-be did not want an Irish band breaking into the scene there.'

Promoter Phil Solomon firmly believed showbands would be the next craze in England and tried to usher in the new era. The band was given major exposure on TV and Top of the Pops, but then something happened which transformed the whole music scene.

The little known band, who had played relief to The Royal Showband in Liverpool a few years previously, had finally found fame, and in doing so, helped bring about the downfall of the showbands.

'The Beatles came and sunk everything,' says Eamonn Monahan. 'When they came along, young fellows wanted to buy guitars. Along came Freddie and the Dreamers, The Tremeloes and hundreds more. The showbands went.'

Country and western music was also creeping in.

'A fellow can become passable with a guitar and a bit of amplification,' says Monahan, 'but ask him to blow a chorus and it's a different story. Country and western music is easily played. These new fellows couldn't blow their nose. There were very few Paddy Coles around.'

Meanwhile, large financial carrots were being dangled in front of Butch Moore. Promises of international stardom and unlimited earnings were made. The Capitol was like an anchor around his neck, he was told.

Butch finally left The Capitol in the summer of '66, signalling the end of an era. Des Kelly and the rest of the band were shocked by his resignation. 'He didn't know how to tell us because he was such a gentle fellow,' Kelly said later.

The move fell flat for Moore, but it had major consequences for those he left behind.

For a time he tried the cabaret scene backed by a trio, but it was very early days in that style of entertainment. People still expected to see and hear a brass section too.

'It just wasn't the same thing at all,' says Cole.

Moore later tried to re-enter the showband scene as a guest star with The Kings, but it was a far cry from the heydays of The Capitol.

'Musically,' says Cole, 'The Kings were excellent, under the direction of Barry Closkey of the present Closkey/Hopkins jazz band, but it was over for Butch, as the scene had changed.'

Eventually, Moore left Ireland. He was broke, but managed to carve out a successful career playing the Irish bars in the States with his new wife, Maeve Mulvaney.

Butch Moore was replaced in The Capitol in May 1966 by a new singer, Noel McNeil from Dublin. 'Noel was a good-looking guy, and a great mover,' says Cole. 'He sang a lot of Tom Jones numbers.'

His first night with The Capitol was in The Television Club.

'Noel was very nervous and had rehearsed for weeks. When he arrived the fans were already ten deep in the hall. So uptight was he that he saluted a couple of guard dogs on the way in.'

But, unknown to the band, McNeil was a homosexual, a fact which he had hidden all his life from the showbusiness fraternity.

When the story was about to leak to the media, he went and told the band management, leaving The Capitol voluntarily in May 1967.

'It must have been tragic for him, given the double life he was leading,' says Cole. 'On stage he was expected to be a womaniser and had to go through this charade every night. People then were obviously not as open-minded as they are today. Later I worked in Vegas with several guys who were gay and it made no difference. In fact Noel used to come in to see us there when I was with The Big 8. I also went to see him sing several times in London. He was one of the nicest guys to work with in the business. It really was tragic.'

Noel McNeil died, a victim of the Aids virus, in late 1994 while still in his 40s.

McNeil was replaced by a popular, Edinburgh-born musician, John Drummond, who was recommended by Phil Coulter.

'Drummond had no idea of the geography of Ireland,' says Cole, 'and he had this dreadful habit of waking up in the wagon just when we were all falling asleep and asking the driver, Seamus McCabe: "Seamus, where are we now?" When we were driving back to Dublin from Cork, Seamus would say "Ballinasloe" and Drummond would say "Good", and happily go back to sleep.' John Drummond is now one of the top bass guitar players in the country, appearing regularly on TV and in musical productions.

As country and western music became more and more the rage, The Capitol seized the opportunity with Des Kelly recording *The Streets of Baltimore*, a song which stayed in the charts for 15 weeks.

'I was quietly delighted with myself,' said Kelly later. 'In my position as band leader, you never got a chance to fly your own flag. I felt my job was to get the best out of other people.'

However, Des Kelly was to be surpassed by his brother Johnny, whose recording of *The Black Velvet Band*, at the suggestion of long-time friend Eddie Masterson, was a runaway success.

Columnist and DJ Ken Stewart wrote at the time: 'As a record reviewer my life is punctuated every once in a while by a record I hear and instantly and instinctively know that not only do I want to personally put out flags in its honour, but also that it is about to become a very big hit . . . . Such a feeling came over me when I slipped a single on the turntable and heard the first few bars of *The Black Velvet Band*. It has to be a giant.'

But the last days of The Capitol were looming.

Des Kelly suffered a bad attack of pneumonia in 1969 and left the band he had helped to found. His brother, Johnny, left the following year.

'Butch Moore was never really replaced,' says Eamonn Monahan. 'Jimmy Hogan and myself left and started The Cabaret All Stars with Mike Short and Kevin Brady. We were doing a nice act, but as the ballad scene came in I got out when a business offer came up.'

The end of The Showband Era was brought about by a number of factors. Country music was emerging as the new attraction, and cabaret venues were opening up where people could relax in comfort. The showbands blamed the ballroom owners, and the owners blamed the showbands for cutting the length of their shows.

'Really what happened,' says RTE's Ronan Collins, who was a drummer with Dickie Rock and his band, 'was the country moved on. Nothing stays the same, and nothing lasts for ever. I would blame the band management and the ballroom owners for not being very far-sighted. And, of course, musicians being musicians are lousy business men. I never met one who didn't think it would last forever whether the show was good, bad or indifferent.'

Gay Byrne puts much of the blame on the ballroom owners.

'The owners were happy to put up these big barns, with a front door, a back door and a cash box. That was about it. I've heard so many of the showband people like Eileen Reid, Twink, Maxi and other girls complain about the appalling conditions in these places. There was no consideration for the performers. There were only toilets, and very basic ones at that, for the clients and often the girls in the showbands had to put on their make-up and get ready in the women's toilet.

'Gradually with the advent of television, people were looking at better things and realised there were places like cabaret venues which were warm and clean. You could order a drink and enjoy a show at the same time. I think the ballroom managers brought about their own demise, and the showbands probably began to price themselves out of it as well. The two things converged and when the lines crossed on the graph, that was the end of that.'

The last remaining members of The Capitol Showband were Paddy Cole and Bram McCarthy. They were joined by Frankie Murray, guitar; Mike Dalton, bass; Eamon Donnelly, drums; Stan Byrne, sax; and Tony O'Leary on vocals. Jim Hand had now taken over as manager.

'Jim got a phone call one day from a guy saying he had heard a fellow, called Tony O'Leary singing, and he was brilliant. He recommended him for The Capitol. "OK, get him to ring me," said Hand, and rang off.

'Tony arrived for audition and got the job. It later emerged it was Tony himself who had made the telephone call to Jim Hand!

'It was funny being on stage with Tony because he had very bad eyesight, but did not want to wear glasses on stage. I'd be performing there beside him, and suddenly he would turn to me and say: "Paddy, are there many in the hall?"

The Capitol continued to tour the States and Canada. While in Toronto, Cole received an invitation to the opening of a new pub in New York owned by an old Castleblaney friend, Frank McElroy. He flew to New York and picked up a cab to go to the Bronx. On the way up Fifth Avenue Cole spotted journalist and friend Michael Hand walking alone along the packed sidewalk.

'Pull in here!' yelled an excited Cole at the cab-driver.

Out he jumped and ran up beside the unsuspecting Hand.

'Begod Mickser, there must be a fair on today, there's such a big crowd around,' declared Cole. Hand was delighted to see his old friend on the ever-crowded Fifth Avenue.

A few days later a report appeared in the *Sunday Independent* on Paddy Cole's greeting of Michael Hand in New York, and his speculation that it must have been a Fair day!

Tony O'Leary was a finalist in The National Song Contest in 1969.

'I remember being out at the rehearsals with Tony when all the fuss was being made of this group, Maxi, Dick and Twink. They were having their photos taken against every setting — in a doorway, beside fast cars and in the shrubbery. There was this very quiet girl sitting in the corner of the room. Her name was Dana, but nobody paid much heed to her. She won both The National Song Contest and The Eurovision.'

On the night of The National Song Contest, The Capitol were playing in Kiltomer, outside Ballinasloe, Co. Galway.

'I insisted that Tony come down there after he had performed on the Song Contest, win, lose or draw. That was always my motto — the gig comes first. To this day I always insist that, even if a car breaks down, the musician gets to the venue by whatever means possible. You have got to make it to the gig. Full stop.

'But on that particular night I thought there would be a huge welcome for Tony after his TV appearance. He arrived very tired and late and there was not much of a crowd anyway. Nobody really cared whether he came or not. I was wrong to insist that he travel all that journey down.'

Drummer Eamon Donnelly also suffered the wrath of Cole.

'We were at the stage when the crowd was dwindling and you always took it out on somebody. The natural person to blame is the drummer — the beat is not right. I lectured away. Eamon should have told me where to get off, but he was too nice a guy.'

By now Des Kelly was managing country bands, including Sweeny's Men, and later The Smoky Mountain Ramblers. His brother Johnny joined him and managed the Virginians. Later both went into the pub business.

Country music was taking over, but Paddy Cole found it uninteresting and unexciting.

'We were at the end of a roll, and we didn't realise it. The takings went down and the crowds dwindled. Then you saw your true friends. Suddenly fellows who had been all over you didn't want to know you.

I remember starting to manage a young band called The Manhattans and I went to a certain promoter in Dublin to try and get gigs for them. He was opening windows in the ballroom with a long pole, but never stopped doing this while I was talking to him. I had to keep walking along to talk to him. It was one of the most degrading things that ever happened to me. I have never forgotten it. I promised myself that I would never let that happen to me again.

'I had played for this guy with The Capitol in their heyday, and when I came back with The Big 8 this fellow and others were all over us again. Maybe that's business generally. Everyone wants to know a winner, and it's the same with the punters, but at the time it was a bitter pill to get a complete deadner from two or three promoters whom I had known very well.

'Towards the end of my days with The Capitol we played in Wexford for a promoter who always waited for us and gave us a few beers, but on this particular night he packed up with a half an hour to go, and drove away home.

'That's showbusiness. You treat it as just that, a business, and if you find a few friends along the way, that's a bonus. But I could count on one hand the true friends I have out of the business. I have many acquaintances, but few personal friends.'

Life got tougher for the band now, travelling in a band wagon on poor country roads. 'One Christmas Day we were booked to play in Carndonagh, Co. Donegal. We were living in Taney Crescent and Santa Claus arrived as usual and the kids were flying around the house, but because of the length of the journey we had to leave for Donegal at 12 noon. Arrangements had been made that we would eat in a local hotel before the gig.

'We arrived in Carndonagh in the frost and snow, and set up the equipment. Later we called to the hotel for our meal, but there was no response. Eventually a fellow, who had obviously been on the beer all day, stuck his head out an upstairs window.

"Who the hell are you?" he yelled.

"We're The Capitol Showband, we're here for our meal," replied Cole.

"There's no meal for any band here. Get to fuck away with yourselves." And with that he slammed the window shut.

'We ended up having sandwiches and tea out of a huge black teapot at the back of the stage. That was our dinner on Christmas Day.'

By the beginning of 1971 The Capitol were forced to hire a wagon. They rushed to get back to Dublin and unload it so as not to be charged for an extra day. It was now a struggle for survival.

The band played in Killarney before going on two weeks' holidays.

'Bram McCarthy and I paid the guys out of our own pocket. Although it was not an awful lot, we had no money left for ourselves.'

It was time to put on the thinking cap.

6
ENTERTAINING ELVIS

Royal Showband keyboard player Gerry Cullen was standing in the bar of The Stardust Hotel in Las Vegas. He had dropped in to collect an item from the dressing room and was about to head off for a stroll before the night's three performances when he suddenly heard the barman's hushed voice: 'Hey, Gerry, do you see who's standing behind you?'

'Who is it?' asked Cullen, not bothering to turn round.

'It's Elvis!' whispered the barman.

'Would you ever fuck off, Elvis my arse!' retorted Cullen.

'I'm telling you, it's Elvis Presley, he's right behind you,' insisted the barman.

Cullen turned around. There, indeed, stood Elvis Presley. He was dressed immaculately, and accompanied by four bodyguards.

'Ah . . . Jaysus . . . Elvis . . . howy'a,' blurted a stunned Cullen.

Just at that moment a woman in her seventies walked up to Elvis and shyly asked the idol for his autograph for her niece.

Elvis smiled. 'For you, honey, I would sign anything,' he declared. With that he signed his name, and gave the woman a hug and a kiss.

'I was very impressed by the incident and I always remembered it,' says Cullen. 'I thought he did it with such style and elegance.'

Cullen introduced himself.

'Elvis, I'm Gerry Cullen. 'I'm a member of The Royal showband, the resident band here in the bar.'

'I know,' said Elvis. 'I'm coming to see your last show tonight. I've met that big guy in your band that takes me off all the time.'

A crowd had suddenly started to gather around the star and his bodyguards swiftly moved him away.

Gerry Cullen was astounded. For many years a highlight of The Royal Showband's performance was the Elvis Presley medley performed by Brendan Bowyer. The Waterford singer was able to do an uncanny take-off of Elvis and the fans at home loved it. The fans in Vegas loved it even more.

Now Gerry Cullen faced a dilemma — whether or not to warn Bowyer and the band that Elvis would be coming in for the last show. He was afraid the star's presence might make Bowyer nervous and upset the act.

When the first hour-long show finished Cullen walked into the dressing room with the rest of the band.

'Lads, you know what, I met Elvis himself this evening,' he declared. Everyone laughed. Some reckoned Cullen had hit the vodka bottle big time again.

'I'm not drunk and I'm not joking,' insisted Cullen. 'He's coming to the last show tonight.'

When the band finally took him seriously, Bowyer began to panic. Before the third show started, it was obvious that a VIP was about to arrive. The media came in their dozens. Heavy security guards were spread all over the hall. A special blacked out booth was set up at the back of the hall. The show went ahead. Bowyer was noticeably nervous, but got through the act without a hitch. As the applause rang out, a spotlight suddenly beamed in on the darkened booth, and there was Elvis, breaking his sides laughing. He had loved every minute of it. As the crowd turned to him, his bodyguards moved in and the star was gone in a flash.

Later a messenger arrived with an invitation from Elvis to visit him in his penthouse suite.

'We all went to visit him, and found him to be a real gentleman,' says Cullen. 'All he wanted to know was about Ireland, although I don't think he knew exactly where it was.'

Two months later Elvis paid the band an unexpected, return visit. He arrived incognito, dressed in a black cape and hood and carrying a cane. Nobody recognised the mystery figure in the front of the hall.

Suddenly, as Brendan Bowyer was about to start his Elvis routine, the real Elvis stood up and shouted: 'Hey you! You're stealing my act!' Then was gone.

'Elvis had a good sense of humour and was a bit of a prankster,' says Cullen.

Later Paddy Cole and The Big 8 would also become friends of the rock n' roll star. 'We visited Elvis when his dressing room was decked out like a gymnasium,' says Cole. 'There were bicycles, rowing machines, treadmills, every aid to keep him fit.'

The Royal had proved a remarkable success in Las Vegas, where they played to largely American–Irish audiences.

They had already clocked up several successful tours of the United States, arranged through promoter Bill Fuller, before he put them in touch with Vegas promoter Rocky Sennes. Their first audition was in Caesar's Palace at three in the afternoon.

'The wife of our trumpeter, Eddie Sullivan, was expecting twins back home and Eddie had left the telephone number of the Palace for contact,' says Cullen. 'We were hanging around until Sennes, a small guy smoking a huge cigar, arrived.

'He stood in the middle of the hall and roared: "Start!" Just as we were heading into the first number the telephone rang and TJ Byrne whispered from the side: "Two boys". Eddie Sullivan was all excited and found it hard to concentrate.'

The cigar-carrying agent became annoyed.

'Hey, guys, what the hell's wrong with you up there,' he yelled.

The band explained that the trumpeter's wife had just given birth to twin boys back in Ireland.

'Congratulations,' said Sennes, 'now do the fuckin' number!'

Afterwards he told them: 'You got the job, guys — for six weeks' and with that he ordered six bottles of champagne for the band.

Cullen attributes a major portion of their success to the fact that they were real Irish musicians, not American–Irish.

'The papers gave us very good write-ups as genuine Irish musicians. This was something new and fresh. We brought over four "Irish" dancers with full choreography. Rocky Sennes agreed a six-month contract and we were in The Stardust for five years.'

For their first stay, The Royal had second billing. Topping the bill were The Supremes. Then there was a group called The Happy Jesters, who performed comedy and slapstick, and finally, they had Jimmy Durante.

The band flew out to Vegas after Christmas and returned in early July.

It was a world very far removed from the Irish ballroom circuit but The Royal managed to crack it because, as Paddy Cole sees it, 'they gave the people what they wanted. They didn't try to be Tony Bennett or Frank Sinatra. They gave the audience a touch of Irish music, a little country and western, some pop. It was a great cross-section, and they ended up being the top act on the Strip.'

The Royal opened their show with Elvis' *Viva Las Vegas*, featuring four girl dancers. There were ten minutes of Irish songs, including *Galway Bay* and *Hannigan's Hooley*. Their brass material went down well with the audience and they adopted *Spanish Flea* as their signature tune.

Bowyer attributed much of their success to the four dancers. He told reporter BP Fallon: 'The Dixies or The Clippers could make it big there on their comedy, while we did it on our spectacular approach. The girls brought great colour to our act.'

When the band sang The Beach Boys' *Sloop John B*, the girls dressed up in cute sailor uniforms. For the Irish numbers they wore green. It was very effective. Only one of the girls was Irish, Phil Cahill from Dublin. She taught the other three, who were American, how to do Irish jigs.

Bowyer also gave a stirring rendition of *Boulavogue*, a song which once caused some English girls performing in a nearby theatre to object to it, on the grounds that it caused racial hatred.

'One of the reasons I think we made it in Vegas,' says Gerry Cullen, 'was because we were ordinary guys, who went over there and got friendly with barmen, hotel taxi-drivers, porters, and others who helped promote us. They accepted us very quickly.'

The Royal succeeded were hundreds more failed. British entertainer Tommy Steele brought his successful show *Half a Sixpence* to Vegas, but it flopped because the audience could not understand the accent.

The band members also enjoyed the good life. In February 1964 Gerry Cullen, Eddie Sullivan, Charlie Matthews and manager TJ Byrnes went to Miami to watch the first fight between Sonny Liston and Cassius Clay (Mohammed Ali).

'We were ringside for the fight, which I still think was a fix,' says Cullen. 'To be there was one of the highlights of my life. Liston failed to come out after the seventh round. We even managed to send messages home through Eamon Andrews who was doing a live commentary for Radio Éireann beside us.'

Liston ended his days working in The Stardust Hotel in Vegas, which was reputedly owned by the mafia. He became very friendly with the members of The Royal Showband.

'He had a beautiful home beside the ninth tee on The Stardust Golf Club,' Cullen recalls. 'We used to play early in the morning, and by the time we got to the ninth, Sonny would be sitting there on the balcony, shouting: "Hi Irish, you guys want a beer?" Suddenly Sonny wasn't there anymore. He was actually dead in the house for days before we knew it. The circumstances surrounding his death are still a mystery.'

The nightly grind was gruelling for the musicians. They played the same tunes and sang the same songs three times a night, six nights a week.

'In the end it helped to break up the band. It was like going into a factory every afternoon.'

Relations deteriorated, and the musicians stayed apart, except for the shows. They rarely spoke to each other.

'It was the worst three months of my life,' says Cullen. 'You were there smiling at the crowd, but the minute you finished, you just got out as fast as you could. In my opinion there were too many outside forces trying to break up the band. It was obvious there was something new being planned by Brendan Bowyer and Tom Dunphy. There was a lot of hurt there. It was sad that seven guys who had gone to school together in Waterford, and started playing together in tennis clubs, but were now big stars in Ireland and the United States, were finally breaking up, but maybe it was time.'

Back in Dublin in 1970, Paddy Cole got a phone call from agent Mick Quinn — who had sold Paddy his first new beetle some years before — saying Brendan Bowyer and Tom Dunphy were leaving The Royal Showband and setting up a totally new band. They wanted Cole in as band leader.

'A company called Tribune, which was set up by Noel Pearson, Robert McGrattan and Michael Quinn, had offered me all kinds of money to leave The Royal and I thought if I could get Paddy Cole, I might try it,' says Brendan Bowyer.

Tribune had reputedly offered Bowyer a £10,000 lump sum, a Jaguar and £1,000 per week, a tempting offer in the Ireland of 1970. Shortly afterwards, Cole met Tom Dunphy in Bill Fuller's hall in Camden Town while touring with The Capitol.

'I told Tom I wanted to level with him about this call I had from Mick Quinn. I said I didn't want to be involved in anything underhand.'

'I know all about the call,' replied Dunphy, 'but you can forget about it, Paddy, because the whole thing is off. Brendan is staying with the band.' The Royal Showband remained intact.

The issue of Brendan Bowyer's contract with the Tribune organisation eventually ended in court.

A year later the issue arose again. This time Bill Fuller's office rang Cole's home in Taney Road, saying Brendan Bowyer and Tom

Dunphy were forming a new band and wanted Cole in as band leader.

'I said to myself this is like the Rip Kirby series in the *Irish Independent*. Look in tomorrow for the next installment. Is he going to leave, or is he not? I phoned Bill Fuller and he confirmed the boys — Bowyer and Dunphy — would be on to me themselves.'

Cole had a couple of meetings with Brendan Bowyer and Tom Dunphy and The Big 8 was formed in September 1971.

'I had known Paddy for a long time and knew his reputation,' says Bowyer. 'I had seen him on stage many times. I knew him to be a guy who was easy to get on with and very popular. When you're working with someone, you need the whole package. Paddy is the whole package; personality, musical ability, humour, everything.'

The story was big news. 'Break-up of Top Showband' screamed the front page of the *Irish Press* on 6 August,1971. It reported that Paddy Cole would travel around the country with Brendan Bowyer and Tom Dunphy recruiting new talent.

'We are hoping for a good blend of youth and experience in the new band which will revitalise things,' Bowyer told the paper. 'Of course we will be depending a lot on Paddy from the musical aspect.'

Tom Dunphy said the emphasis of the new band would be on good musicianship and strong arrangements.

'What I mean by strong arrangements is that we will try to bring an individual style to the songs we play.'

First, however, Cole had to sever his links with The Capitol.

'Manager Jim Hand, Des Kelly and myself had financed a band called The Ranchers, and they had not done well. I was called in to a meeting with Des Kelly, manager Jim Hand and accountant Denis Byrne and persuaded to sign a document committing me to paying off an outstanding debt of £600, a lot of money at the time. But I managed to do it. I was also offered jobs in other bands. Guitarist Jimmy Hogan had joined Brendan Shine, and told me

Brendan would be looking for a sax player, but it was not really my sort of music.'

As band leader with The Big 8, Paddy Cole set out to hand-pick a team of top musicians. The new band would combine the experience of Bowyer and Dunphy with the talent of Cole and other top class musicians. It would be the cream of Irish musicians in one unit.

Drummer Micky O'Neill, who had replaced Johnny Kelly in the Capitol, and subsequently left to join the Swarbriggs, was brought in. The move caused some bad feelings.

'We went to The National Ballroom to see Micky, and the Swarbrigg brothers got suspicious. Micky assured them there was no problem. Later that night O'Neill phoned Cole from the Swarbriggs' home where there was a major row going on.

'The brothers felt I had poached Micky. I got the name of being the Big Bad Wolf.'

Former Capitol guitarist Jimmy Hogan agreed to join, and had photographs taken with the new line-up, but was held to his contract with The Spotlights by manager Tom Doherty. Jimmy Conway came in as guitarist. Conway suggested Twink as a female vocalist and she, too, agreed to sign up.

The full line-up of The Big 8 was: Brendan Bowyer, vocals and trombone; Tom Dunphy, vocals and bass; Twink, vocals; Paddy Cole, sax and clarinet; Dave Coady (ex-Real McCoy), trumpet; Jimmy Conway (ex-The Strangers), guitar; Micky O'Neill, drums; and Michael Keane (ex-Johnny McEvoy), piano. TJ Byrne, who had left The Royal some time previously, took over as manager.

The Royal Showband continued under the management of Connie Lynch, but not for long. The departure of Bowyer and Dunphy had a traumatic effect, and the band broke up within a year.

After intensive rehearsals, The Big 8 was launched in Manchester and did a tour of England and Ireland before flying out to Vegas. The reaction at home was terrific. Bowyer was at his peak and the music was top class. Thousands again poured into the ballrooms, attracted by the outfit of top names.

Members of The Big 8 Showband pictured in Evansville, Indiana in 1974. Back row: (from left) Micky O'Neill (drums), Jimmy Conway (guitar). Front row: Paddy Cole (sax), Tom Dunphy (bass guitar) and Dave Coady (trumpet).

'The Big 8 was a sensational band,' says Bowyer. 'The showband era was waning but we had the cream of the musicians and the Las Vegas contract.'

In Vegas The Big 8 took where The Royal had left off. They used the same format and had a heavy Irish flavour in their programme. For the Vegas show, four glamorous dancers were added to the band — lead dancer Rita Houlihan, Phyllis O'Brien, Angela Larney and Maureen Carter. Paddy Cole played the tin whistle and the girls danced jigs and reels.

At the end of the show, when the band played rock 'n' roll, the girls adapted to Go Go dancing. It was a totally professional act.

Bowyer continued his Elvis act with stirring interpretations of numbers such as *Jailhouse Rock* and *Hound Dog*.

For Paddy Cole, Las Vegas was a totally new experience. Although he had toured the States many time with The Capitol, he had never been there.

'I will always remember the first night we flew in,' he says. 'Tom Dunphy had hoped it would be night time because the scene from the aeroplane was spectacular. I had never seen anything like it. The planes used to deliberately fly up the Strip for the view. Dunphy had told me that if you go there once, you will always want to return.'

Paddy's wife, Helen — they had married in 1965 — moved out to Vegas as well, and they rented an apartment just off the Strip. In Vegas everything ran — and still runs — round the clock, 24 hours a day, seven days a week.

'The pubs,' says Cole, 'had no windows and looked the same at 3a.m. as they did at 3p.m. There were no clocks anywhere. Our "local" was The Flame. It was owned by a guy of Italian extraction, Bill Laruso. Bill wanted desperately to be Irish, and was known to his Irish customers as Liam O'Laruso. The Flame was a dangerous temptation for us. We'd finish our last show at around 3a.m. and head to the Flame for a few drinks. Often, when we left, the sun would hit you in the face. Only then would we realise it was 7a.m.! We would be waiting to be put out, like at home, but of course, that never happened in Vegas. It got to the stage where we had to discipline ourselves, and say: "I've got to leave now". Being honest about it, there were an awful lot of times we didn't.'

Paddy and his wife, Helen on their wedding day on 27 February 1965.

Paddy made friends with an Irish/American scientist, Ronnie Scanlon, who worked on space test sites in the desert. His father had been a policeman in New York.

'Ronnie had never been to Ireland, but as he got more beer into him, he would acquire an Irish accent, and the mist would start to come down over Ben Bulben! These guys were more Irish than the Irish. Ronnie was very good to us.'

When The Big 8 arrived in Vegas, they were told there were two Irish societies in the city. One was the Friendly Sons of St Patrick, which mainly represented successful Irish/American business-men. The Big 8 were invited to join them.

'We were also warned about the second society, the Sons of Erin. One of the casino bosses, Tommy Callaghan, warned us that the meetings of this society were just a cover for drinking sessions. We headed straight for the Sons of Erin!'

Events at home provided cause for the over-indulgence.

'When word came through that Helen had given birth to our daughter, Karen, there was great excitement and wild celebrations. Fellows ended up in hospital after it. Dave Coady rode a motor-bike through a wall! Jimmy Conway dived into a swimming-pool with no water!

Dave Coady still carries the scars of the incident, a bent finger. Every time he sees me, he points the finger at me and asks: "How is that kid of yours?" '

The monotony of the routine and the drinking excesses caused some of the band, including Bowyer, to fall victim to the booze and become alcoholics. The after-effects of the drinking splurges led to depression.

'I remember sitting on a park bench one night and wondering when could I get the next flight out of the place,' says Cole.

The Big 8 continued to pack The Stardust for the thrice nightly shows. Also featured with them on the programme was a group of topless girls, called The Bare Touch of Vegas.

'In the beginning we would be walking along the corridor when we would meet these girls with very little on. Our eyes used to be out on sticks looking at them, but in the end it became so much a part of the routine, we didn't take a blind bit of notice of them! Nor were there any secret affairs going on behind the spotlights.

'Despite the obvious assumption,' says Twink, 'there was never, and I mean never, any hanky-panky between the band members or the dancing girls. At the time I was coming out of a relationship with Jimmy Conway. Over the years when Paddy and I travelled so much together people used to gossip, but we were always just the best of friends. It made life easier when it was just a good working relationship, and that is how it has remained.'

The arrival of Twink posed a new challenge for the four female dancers as there had never been a girl singer in the act before. Twink solved the problem by leaving the dressing room to the girls, and using a little annex room for herself.

When one of the dancers, Dubliner Angela Larney, saw Twink's date of birth, she was not impressed.

'Holy Jaysus, girls,' she declared, 'did you see your wan's birth date? SHE was born in the fuckin' 50s. All we need here now is a bloody college girl. And where doz SHE think she's going with dat accent?'

But Paddy reassured Twink that, despite the critical reception, she would be fine and eventually she ended up sharing an apartment with Phyllis O'Brien.

'There was always the annual battle for the upstairs apartments,' adds Twink, 'so that you wouldn't have the lizards and other creepy-crawly things blowing in under your front door.'

The band usually headed to Vegas a few weeks before wives and partners, and they displayed the traditional Irishman's helplessness when it came to feeding themselves.

'They didn't understand the meaning of self-catering,' says Twink. 'Some of them availed of the 89 cents breakfast, the $1.25 lunch somewhere else, with spare ribs somewhere else again for dinner.

They also had their admirers. Among them were the women of the legendary Lido de Paris show, whose basic requirement was that they must be at least six feet tall.

'Hi Irish, these Amazon women used to say to me,' says Twink. 'What is the crack tonight? And then they would walk past with their legs up to their elbows, make-up removed by Let O'Brien Shift It and hair by Scafco. Still they were a sight to behold and all these really tall, glamorous girls with the big tits and small asses, were mad about the Irish boys, and particularly Paddy, because of his height and personality.'

The band usually had Tuesday free and after the last show on Monday night Paddy and Helen would head off to the Hoover dam on the Colorado river. There a friend of The Big 8 would leave a boat and some fishing gear ready for them.

'We would try and be there for 5.30a.m. and go trout fishing for the morning. We had to be off the river by 11a.m. because of the intense heat. It was a notorious spot for drowning because the water, which came down from the mountains, was ice-cold despite the very high temperatures. People who fell into the river often could not make it to the shore because they froze to death.'

The intense heat caused problems for the Irish visitors, unused to such excesses.

'We bought cheap cars over there, but you had to be careful to make sure they had refrigeration. Air conditioning was no good because you were only blowing in more hot air. Once, on a picnic with Helen and the kids, the cooling mechanism broke down and we all nearly died from heat exhaustion. As we were gasping and picking up drinks anywhere we could, we saw the old pioneer trails where explorers had first come out in covered wagons. How they survived I'll never understand.'

The rain came just once when they were there, and it was torrential. 'Everywhere was flooded with mud on the streets. They did not have adequate rain gully to take the water. I used to get up in the morning at around 11.30, but the day it rained Helen called me at 9.30. And there we stood, like two schoolchildren, gazing for hours at the rain. There were times it was so hot, I wished I was standing at a street corner in Castleblaney in the lashing rain. A doctor once told us it took six months for the bloodstream to become acclimatised to the hot weather, and the same when you returned home. So our bodies were going through permanent torture. It was tough going.'

But there were compensations, like a meeting with every boy's cowboy hero, Roy Rogers.

'One night, after a show in The Stardust, this guy came up to Tom Dunphy and said he had Roy Rogers outside, and it was Roy Rogers. I was in awe of this guy, but he invited me out for a drink. We had a hell of a night on the town. I told him about going to see his films in the Four Pennies in Castleblaney.' One night became two, and two became three. Helen Cole was not impressed by all this late night carousing, even with Roy Rogers. Soon Paddy Cole, too, had had enough.

The late *Sunday World* editor, Kevin Marron, arrived in Vegas to write some articles and was staying in the Coles' apartment. Suddenly the telephone rang. 'Helen, if that's Roy Rogers, tell him I'm not here,' declared a determined Paddy Cole. Marron almost collapsed off the sofa with disbelief.

Years later, when Kevin Marron was killed tragically in an air crash on the Beaujolais run to France, Paddy Cole attended his funeral in Dundalk.

'I was outside the door of the Cathedral when I heard this burst of laughter inside. Fr Brian D'Arcy had told the story during the homily. Later, Paddy O'Hanlon of the SDLP, a good friend of mine, rang to say he wished he had been the guy who had said those words to Marron.'

On their nights off, the band got complimentary tickets to the other shows on the Strip. They regularly went to see Frank Sinatra or Elvis Presley.

'But I was always struck by the number of very talented comedians, singers and artists of all kinds that you never heard of again. Many of them were top class, but they never made it because it was such a rat race. Many are now bartenders in and around Vegas.'

Frequently Paddy and Helen Cole just went to a movie, to get away from the Vegas scene.

Cole got a unexpected surprise when an old acquaintance from Dublin, Shan Wilkinson, who had been a band leader, arrived in town. He had gone to live in Hawaii where he had joined the Don Howe orchestra, a major attraction in the Pacific.

'Shan had gone into the museum in Hawaii and studied the old percussion instruments of the region. He had them rebuilt exactly and finished up being a top percussionist.'

Gambling was everywhere in Vegas. Some casinos were the size of Croke Park. When you went to the supermarket, there was even a machine at the checkout to gamble your small change. When you lined up to go to a show, you lined up beside the slot machines. You went to the bar for a drink and there were gambling machines there, too. There were even gambling machines in the toilets. And, as with drink, some of the musicians became addicts and paid a high price.

Twink made a real impact on stage in Vegas.

'She did a first class act singing numbers like *I've Got a Brand New Pair of Roller Skates*. She used to skate across the stage while singing and it was clear that her forte was to be an actress in musical shows. The song made such an impact that fellows used to come up to her with pairs of roller skates. Today Twink still has an attic full of roller-skates to prove it.'

'I have a gold necklace with a roller-skate on it,' says Twink. I have a bracelet with gold roller-skates on it. They even had a special boot made in gold for me, roller-skate and all.' Then Twink would demonstrate her versatility by coming out on stage in a full length gown and singing *I Don't Know How to Love Him* from Jesus Christ Superstar. At the time, Andrew Lloyd Webber was only breaking into the United States. Her performance used to bring the house down.

Twink and Brendan Bowyer never hit it off together, and had frequent rows. 'Brendan was the boss,' says Cole. 'If a show was running over, he would have to make a decision on what numbers were to be cut, and Twink would often be left sitting back stage.'

She was infuriated.

'Night after night, he would cut more of my stuff out to the point where I thought he just brought me on to humiliate me. I would stand there and sing nothing. I might have people in to see me but Brendan would tell me not to bother coming on at all. "Twink, I've some people coming in tonight and they have requested that I sing *Galway Bay* myself", he used to say to me. Bowyer is one of my least favourite people on earth. "Your ticket is in the drawer," used to be a great line of his.'

As band leader, Paddy Cole's job was to mediate and try to keep the peace. He could sympathise with how Twink felt.

'Often I had to comfort Twink after a show when the dancers would call me in and tell me she was crying. I had to explain to her that everyone had some numbers cut,' he says.

'Paddy knew the torment I was going through,' says Twink. 'Basically Bowyer regretted bringing a woman into the front line. Paddy used to say to me: "Twink, you haven't even tasted the icing on the cake yet. Forget about it. You haven't started your career yet".'

Despite the show's success, Bowyer was always very uptight.

'When we finished and went to the dressing rooms, there was always a post mortem,' Cole recalls. 'He was a perfectionist. We would get a standing ovation as the revolving bandstand turned at the end of the night, but still Brendan would not be happy and would want to tighten up here or there. He never left anything to chance.'

The band was owned by Bowyer and Dunphy. Tom Dunphy was the business head and made all the financial arrangements.

'He was reared in the Kerry Gaeltacht and whenever he was counting he would have to do it in Irish. So there he used to be in the middle of Las Vegas going: "A haon déag, a dó dhéag, a trí déag . . . . ".'

Twink blamed Bowyer, not Dunphy, for the rows that developed.

'The line I was fed from senior sources was that Bowyer made the balls for Tom Dunphy to fire,' she says. 'To me Tom was a gentleman. I was crazy about him, and loved him passionately. He was a beautiful man and to this day I miss his companionship. I miss the odd call he would give me when in Dublin. We used to stay up until all hours discussing philosophy and life. He was just a super person. I was heartbroken when he was killed.'

Manager TJ Byrne stirred things up by telling somebody that The Big 8 were considering buying one of the major Vegas venues, the Circus Circus Casino. 'One of the Irish papers heard about this and rang Circus Circus management to ask if it was true,' said Cole. There was consternation. You could not buy the place for a hundred million, even then. The management of the hotel had an SOS out for TJ Byrne. We nearly ended up in court over his off-the-cuff remark.

'There were a lot of rumours as to who was running the hotel as the mafia were heavily involved in Vegas. TJ had to sweat it out for a while in case these boys would come after him. And at home, the taxman began to wonder how The Big 8 could be in a position to buy a multi-million pound hotel!

Back in Ireland for six months, The Big 8 continued to draw in big crowds.

'Before gigs Brendan Bowyer used to say to me: "Paddy, the people are fed up of *The Hucklebuck*". I used to have to force him to do it every night. But as soon as we started into the first few bars, the place erupted. They loved it as much as ever, but it's hard to psyche yourself all the time.'

The Coles had long decided that Vegas would not be a permanent way of life for them. They wanted to rear their three children in Ireland. For them, family came first. They were worried, too, about the drug culture.

'Drugs were one of the reasons we left Vegas. The pushers used to give out sweets with drugs to schoolchildren, to get them hooked. To me there is something odd about a guy sitting on his own, smoking a joint and getting high as a kite. For me drinking a pint is about having a chat and a laugh. In Ireland you can never go into a pub without striking up a conversation with somebody.'

TJ Byrne and Paddy Cole pictured in Las Vegas with the former World heavy-weight boxing champion, Joe Louis.

The monotony of the three-times-a-night show was also getting to Paddy Cole. 'There was also a difference of opinion between Brendan Bowyer and Tom Dunphy, who jointly owned the band, as to whether we should live permanently in Vegas. I supported going home, but I could see the thing swaying, and a situation arising where we might be living there permanently. That certainly was not our plan. At that stage of the game we realised Las Vegas was a tinsel city with a very transient population. You had no great friends because once you got to know somebody, suddenly they moved on again.'

There was also the danger of burn-out for a musician or a band.

'If you went over the hill as an entertainer, or played yourself out, then there was nothing left for you except maybe a job in a garage, or as a waitress.'

The Coles came back to Ireland in the summer of '74 with the intention of going back to Vegas. But they never did.

7
A MASSACRE BY THE ROADSIDE

July 29, 1975. The time: 6.30p.m. Outside the village of Drumsna, Co. Leitrim, a Ford Granada 3000 GXL car is travelling to the village on its way to Donegal when suddenly it collides with a truck. The driver, Tom Dunphy (40), is killed instantly and has to be cut from the wreckage by two units of the Carrick-on-Shannon Fire Brigade. A passenger in the car, Noel Ryan, a fellow member of The Big 8 from Poleberry, Waterford, is taken to Longford Hospital, but is not seriously injured. Both had been on their way to a dance in Dungloe, Co. Donegal, where The Big 8 were due to play.

The showband industry was shocked by the death of Dunphy and went into mourning. The tragic accident received pages of coverage in the daily newspapers. Tributes flowed in from everywhere. There was huge sympathy for his wife Maura and four children, Caroline, then aged fifteen, Terry, aged eleven, eight-year-old Tom Jnr, and Colm, aged three.

Brendan Bowyer had gone to the Galway Races, and then directly to Bundoran. He was having dinner with TJ Byrne in The Great Northern Hotel when he heard the news. Both were stunned.

The other members of the band — trumpeter Dave Coady, drummer Martin Brannigan, lead guitarist Ray Doherty and singer Kelley (formerly of the Nevada) were in The Longford Arms Hotel when they learned of the tragedy.

Paddy Cole, who had recently left The Big 8 to form his own band, had passed Dunphy on the road in Kilbeggan, going in the opposite direction. Cole was about to go on stage in Ballybunion when he heard Dunphy had been killed. He broke the news to Twink.

'We all found it very hard to do the gig that night. Every so often Twink would leave the stage and go for a cry. At the end of the night we announced what had happened and there were people crying all over the hall.'

The dance in Dungloe was cancelled, even though about 1,200 fans had already turned up. Hundreds broke down in tears when they heard the news.

Thirteen showbands were represented at the Dunphy funeral in Tramore on August 1. The pall bearers were members of The Big 8 and The Royal Showband. He had been a founder member of both.

In a tribute, Brendan Bowyer said: 'Tom was one of the finest people I have ever met and his loss echoed around the world. . . . By his talent as an artist and by his kindness and friendliness as an individual, he became an institution in Irish showbusiness. His untimely death has left a void in the hearts of everyone who knew him.'

Twink wrote: 'I feel the world of country music has lost a tremendous talent, and I feel I have lost one of the best friends I ever had.'

In a special tribute a year later, Paddy Cole wrote: 'I knew Tom right through the showband boom days. I had the honour of working with him both at home and in Las Vegas. Tom was a real professional. He could go on stage and really win over the fans with his singing and patter. I often think of him as I'm driving to and from dances. He could sell the act before you played at all. In

Vegas he used to give me such a build-up that I was sold before I even blew a note.'

Three years after his death, his widow Maura unveiled a six foot high memorial at Mohill Cross, near Drumsna, at the spot where he was killed. The piece was sculpted in stone by Jimmy Joe McKiernan from Fenagh, Co. Leitrim.

The death of Tom Dunphy took a heavy toll on The Big 8, and in particular, on Brendan Bowyer. 'Tom was a big loss both on and off the stage,' says Bowyer. 'He was first and foremost, a friend and it took a long time to get over his death. I went to Bill Fuller's hotel in Ballybunion and took what might be termed "an alcohol break".

'I drank an awful lot after his death and kept fooling myself because I was still able to stand up and do the job. I was told by my doctor I was going to die. Seven years later, in 1982, I took a month off and went into a care unit in Vegas. That was the end of my drinking.'

Paddy Cole had left The Big 8 a short time before Tom Dunphy's death. He and Helen had decided that Las Vegas was not for them, and they returned home in the summer of '74. Then a small, but significant, incident happened.

'The Big 8 played at a dance in Virginia, Co. Cavan. Eddie Sullivan, the former trumpeter with The Royal Showband, was driving Micky O'Neill and myself around. After the gig, some showbusiness people whom we knew came back to our hotel and we had a few drinks. It was a motel-style hotel with the bedrooms separate from the main building. Late in the night we went back to the main hotel for a drink but found the place locked. The night porter was asleep and we could not wake him up. We noticed one window slightly open and we slipped in through it. It was the bar, but we were locked into it.'

Each of the late night revellers took turns at serving and they put the money in an ashtray. The story-telling continued until close to 7a.m. when a very surprised manager unlocked the door.

'The manager went bananas, completely over the top. Despite our pleas and the evidence of the money in the ashtray, he said it was not good enough. He announced that he was immediately phoning our manger, TJ Byrne and the gardai to charge us with breaking and entering. So we said to hell with this guy and went into the restaurant to have some breakfast.'

Again the angry manager returned and threatened them with all sorts of charges. Suddenly Micky O'Neill interjected:

'I hope, sir . . . hic . . . you are not accusing us of being . . . hic . . . drunk . . . hic?' he warned the manager with his forefinger. And with that, an inebriated O'Neill awkwardly struck his plate with his fork and toppled his entire fry on to his lap.

'I said to myself, that's us bollixed anyway,' says Cole. 'We were all roaring laughing at nothing and I could hear an elderly American lady saying to her husband: "Hey, Ralph, those three guys over there are drunk. What time of the day is it?"'

The revellers finally retired to get some sleep. When they awoke some hours later, there was a letter from TJ Byrne stating they had brought the band into disrepute.

'This was a totally innocent situation that had been blown out of all proportion. When I saw the contents of the letter, it finally made up my mind for me. I was leaving The Big 8.'

Twink had already left, having grown disillusioned with the Las Vegas routine.

While in Co. Cavan, Paddy had been contacted by Dicky Sullivan, who worked in Top Rank Promotions with Tony Loughman.

'Dicky asked would I be interested in staying at home and putting a band together of my own. As Tony Loughman himself used to put it: "Paddy, we'll get a girl singer and a good playing band behind her." Country and western music was very big at the time.'

On the way to Ballybofey the following day, Paddy Cole told Eddie Sullivan and Micky O'Neill that he was going to start his own band.

'It was not necessarily over the Virginia letter, but it pushed me over the top.'

O'Neill, Michael Keane and Jimmy Conway all asked to join the band. Dave Coady said he wanted to return to Las Vegas.

'I told the lads we'd be starting from the bottom again and they would not be getting all the perks they had enjoyed with The Big 8, including foreign travel. I was finding it hard to cope with the huge enthusiasm from the lads.'

Cole told Tony Loughman he was interested in the project. Loughman was delighted and it was agreed that Cole would approach Twink.

'I'll always remember the day I called over to see Twink. She suffered badly from hay fever and her face was swollen and her eyes streaming. She was in an absolutely dreadful state. We talked for an hour or so and Twink said she was thinking of going into cabaret on her own.'

At the time, Twink had abandoned her singing career and was studying for a riding instructor's exam in England. She was then working as a stable manageress in a riding school in Rathfarnam.

'The day Paddy called I was up to my ears in horse-shite and a troublesome pony and a mother whose child had a fall from the pony. I'd had a really bad day when Paddy Cole walked into the yard.

"Howy'a Gertie?" says he (he always referred to me as "Gertie").'

Cole put it to Twink that she should join his new band as lead female singer. 'One step at a time, sweet Jesus,' replied Twink, 'this is all too much for a white woman. They're ALL leaving The Big 8!

'I told Paddy I was out of showbusiness. I never wanted to to be in it, I never liked it when I was in it, and I did not want to go back into it. I am working with animals now, and when I get this start I'm going back to my books and doing veterinary medicine.

'At that stage I had 13 dogs, 11 cats, two horses and a pony, and I figured I might save a few bills if I knew how to treat my own animals. I was breeding Purenean mountain dogs. Paddy brought me down to the house and put pressure on me to join. He said he had to let the lads on the band know my response that evening at seven o'clock. He said all of them were down in the Old Stand bar with wee Louis Dignam waiting for him.'

Cole waited while Twink changed her clothes, and by 9 o'clock she was talked into joining the new band.

Cole now had five members of the original Big 8. They contacted Pat Morris, a vocalist whom Jimmy Conway knew in Toronto, and he joined up. So, too, did Ray Moore on keyboards and trumpet. He had been with The Plattermen. Mike Dalton joined on bass.

And so The Paddy Cole Superstars were born. The story of The Big 8 split was front page news. A deal was worked out between Cole and Tony Loughman whereby the latter would finance the band and be repaid later by Paddy.

'Tony Loughman was a great man to make a decision. Once he made it, he followed it through. Even to this day, when I have a problem, I say to myself: "Now, how would Tony Loughman sort this one out?"'

There was one job left to do. TJ Byrne, Brendan Bowyer and Tom Dunphy had yet to be told of the new band.

'We were rehearsing in Ennis and preparing for The Rose of Tralee. Suddenly TJ Byrne came in and said he wanted to talk to me. He started to laugh.

"Paddy," he said, "You won't believe this, but a reporter has been on from one of the evening papers wanting me to confirm that you and a few of the lads are leaving the band and going out on your own."

I told him that it was true but that I was not going to say anything until after The Rose of Tralee. I said some of us were simply tired of the Vegas routine.'

TJ Byrne threw his hands in the air.

'Paddy, is your mind made up for definite?'

''Tis TJ,' replied Cole.

Byrne shook hands with him and wished him the best of luck. Then Byrne told Bowyer and Dunphy. The rehearsals were immediately called off and the atmosphere became unpleasant.

'I did not blame the lads. I was raging the way the story had leaked. One of the girls in Tony Loughman's office had inadvertently told somebody that there was a big band being formed. I would not have taken it very well myself had it happened the other way round.'

The story was splashed across the *Evening Herald* and the *Evening Press* on the following day.

The band moved to Tralee and were rehearsing for the first night when in walked a subdued Tom Dunphy.

'Right everyone,' he snapped, 'we're finishing tonight. We've cancelled all the dates for the next few weeks and we're going to reform The Big 8.'

Cole accepted, but insisted those leaving the band get paid for the following three weeks as they had no income. Dunphy snapped that the issue was a matter for the accountants to sort out.

There was one man Paddy Cole dreaded meeting — American promoter Bill Fuller was back in his native Kerry for The Rose of Tralee and was expected to drop in. The speculation was that Fuller would sort out the whole problem. He arrived in the Mount Brandon sooner than expected. He strode up the hall wearing a long trench coat, his hands tightly clenched in his pockets.

'I didn't want to have a confrontation with Fuller because he he was a guy I admired and got on with very well.'

'Patcheen (Fuller always referred to Cole as "Patcheen"), I only want to ask you one thing: Is your mind made up, or can we talk and try to sort this thing out?'

'Yes, Bill,' replied Cole, 'my decision was made mainly for family reasons. It's nothing personal.'

Fuller put out his hand.

'Then the best of luck to you, Patcheen.' And he promised that all the band members would be paid their wages in full.

That night saw the last performance by the original Big 8. It was a special function for promoters and others involved in showbusiness, organised by Frank McCloone.

'The break-up of the band was the talk of the place. There was nothing but wise cracks like: "Keep those fellows well apart". We finished the night, and broke up. I went straight into rehearsals with the new band.

The Paddy Cole Superstars opened in Letterkenny in the summer of 1975. Among the good luck telegrams was one from TJ Byrne, Tom Dunphy, Brendan Bowyer and Dave Coady. It was a nice gesture of goodwill. The Superstars took off very successfully.

'We were liked because we filled a void at the time,' says Twink. 'We weren't quite as *avant garde* as the sort of Chips-type band, who were the best there was, and neither were we country. We were just a really good pop band. Paddy had chosen it very well: Mike Dalton who covered the real country stuff, and Micky O'Neill on drums, who did any of the comedy stuff that was in the charts.

'Of course there was a plethora of women's songs at the time and I covered those. Pat Morris was also a fantastic singer. In the end, it was almost a completely Northern-based band.'

The drill was that a roadie collected the Northern members at a Monaghan base to bring them to gigs, while Cole and Twink travelled from Dublin in Paddy's white Mercedes.

'Today Paddy Cole blames me for getting him back into the business, and I blame him for getting me into comedy while we travelled many thousands of miles together up and down the country. He had an extraordinary genius for telling stories. He was a master story-teller.'

The Superstars toured abroad as well, including a visit to Canada. There they met Pat Hughes and Peter McAleer of Tara Mines.

'One night in a hotel,' Paddy recalls, 'Pat Hughes could not order any drink because it was 3 o'clock in the morning. So he phoned a guy that worked for him and asked him to clear out his fridge and bring in the beer. This guy, we found out later, lived 45 miles away, but he brought in a dozen beer.

The Paddy Cole Superstars. From left: Ray Moore (piano and trumpet), Tony Hughes (vocals and guitar), Twink (vocals), Jimmy Smyth (lead guitar), Pat Sharkey (bass). Seated: Colm Hughes (drums and vocals) and Paddy Cole.

'They had been up in the Yukon and some of the Eskimos gave them presents of delicacies, including reindeer meat, and the penis of a walrus, which is a great honour. Pat Hughes gave me this box of reindeer meat and I was wondering how am I going to go back to the hotel with it. When I arrived back, there was pandemonium when the porters spotted a line of red blood following me across the hallway. The guy who had driven in the 45 miles into town, and was now totally pissed off, was standing nearby. So I said to him: "Here, hold this a minute", and I was gone, leaving the hapless man with the box of bleeding reindeer meat.'

Not long into their new life, The Superstars played in The Tara Club on Westmoreland St., which was owned by Frank McCloone. Brendan Bowyer and Tom Dunphy were among those who came along to see them.

'I was walking down off the stage when I saw Tom Dunphy talking to some people. I nodded to him, but on reflection I should have gone over to shake hands with him. It was the last time I saw him because he was killed shortly after that.'

After Dunphy's funeral in Tramore, Bill Fuller again approached Paddy Cole with a view to rejoining The Big 8. Frank McCloone acted as mediator for the meeting, which took place in The Gresham Hotel. Cole turned down the offer.

'They pleaded with me not to make up my mind until I heard the deal. But I said I didn't want to hear it because there would be winter nights that I'd be playing in paraffin oil halls somewhere down the country and saying why didn't I take it. So I didn't want to know. Furthermore, I could never be quoted about the offer as I never knew what it was.

'They were going to cut me in for a slice of the action in Vegas which would have been very good financially, but the family came first. The kids were settled back into school again in Dublin. If I went back to Vegas I would have been letting the band down. As it transpired, they started to let me down because one by one they left the band.'

Michael Keane, the keyboard player, left to return to The Big 8. So, too, did Jimmy Conway and Micky O'Neill. They missed Vegas and the travel abroad. The Big 8 never successfully filled the void left by Paddy Cole. He was first replaced by Pat Chesters from Omagh, who had played with The Plattermen, and later by Podger Reynolds from Drogheda, who had also replaced Cole in the Maurice Lynch band.

'We never really replaced Cole,' says Bowyer. 'DJ Curtin was the final physical replacement but he has gone in a different direction. He was a good singer but would not be the sax or clarinet player that Paddy was.'

In 1980 The Big 8 moved to The Barbary Coast Hotel and remained there until 1990. Between 1980 and 1985, the band did not return to Ireland at all, and caused a bit of a sensation when they made an appearance at Clontarf Castle in the summer of '85.

These days the current Big 8 divide their time between The Aladdin Hotel in Vegas, The Four Queens Hotel, the Showboat, The Riviera and, of course, the annual trip to Clontarf Castle.

Meanwhile, back in Ireland with his own band, Paddy Cole was settling into a new role with The Superstars.

'If I had contacted Rocky Sennes, I knew we could have gone to Vegas, but I had no interest in going there. The lads were worried about their contracts with Tony Loughman, but I sorted that out and let them off.'

When musicians left, they were replaced by new and better blood.

Colm Hughes came in on drums and his brother Tony, who had fronted his own band, on vocals. 'Wee' Jimmy Smyth replaced Jimmy Conway on guitar as did Micky McCarthy from Castleblaney, who later toured with Johnny Logan after his first Eurovision win, and Pat Sharkey.

'We finished up with a young, vibrant band, very fresh and very musical.'

The Superstars were huge in the North and concentrated their energies there.

'We used to play for Big Brendan Mullgrew in places like Cookstown where there would be 1,200 to 1,400 people gathered before we played a note.

Then came The Miami massacre. In the early hours of Wednesday 31 July, 1975, the Miami Showband completed another successful gig in The Castle Ballroom, Banbridge, Co. Down. The group, now fronted by up-and-coming songwriter/singer Fran O'Toole, was in good spirits as they packed their equipment. Like many other bands, they frequently played in the North. Dickie Rock, The Miami's former lead singer, had left the band three years previously to pursue a solo career.

On the road between Banbridge and Newry, they were stopped by a lone figure waving a red light. Three more men had appeared from behind the hedge wearing combat jackets and berêts and clutching machine guns. The five band members (Ray Miller, the drummer, had gone to his parents' home in County Antrim) were told to put their hands on their heads and face the hedge.

Suddenly there was an explosion just as two of the gunmen were placing a 10 lb bomb in the minibus. It went off prematurely. Band leader, Des Lee — real name Desmond McAlea — was blown through the hedge into a field.

The killers fired indiscriminately as the musicians made a bid for freedom. Fran O'Toole (29), instrumentalist Tony Geraghty (23) and trumpeter Brian McCoy (30), were killed instantly. Des Lee pretended to be dead as he lay stunned in the field. A fourth member, Stephen Travers, was found in the field, critically injured with bullets in his chest and abdomen.

Lee managed to get up and run across the field. He made it to a public road some distance away and flagged down a lorry. The driver took him to Newry police station, five miles away, and he raised the alarm.

Two terrorists, Horace Boyle, a UVF activist from Portadown, and Wesley Somerville, from Caledon, Co. Tyrone, were killed in the explosion.

The dawn revealed the extent of the carnage. Pieces of bloodstained clothing lay on the ground alongside musical instruments, records and photographs.

Dickie Rock had performed at The Seapoint in Galway on the Wednesday night. Just 24 hours earlier, The Miami had been there.

The massacre shocked the showband industry. The ballrooms fell silent as a mark of respect. Paddy Cole was on his way back from The Tara Club on Westmoreland Street where he had been discussing the Tom Dunphy tragedy with Frank McCloone and Connie Lynch, the manager of the Royal Showband, and stopped to pick up a morning paper from a regular news vendor on O'Connell St.

'The fellow told me he'd heard there was some sort of tragedy involving a band on the Border. When I got home I phoned the *Independent* to try and find out what had happened. Tony Wilson, the paper's music correspondent, answered the phone. I knew immediately there was something wrong as it was only 5a.m. and he was already in his office.

'Tony, what's the story?' I asked.

'Paddy, there's been a tragedy. We don't know yet if it was a crash or whatever, but there are showband people dead, and we think it's The Miami. I phoned Connie Lynch and he broke down in tears. Then we then heard the whole awful story.'

After Fran O'Toole's funeral a number of musicians, including Paddy Cole, went out to the RTE studios in Donnybrook to watch a programme featuring him. 'There is no knowing where Fran might have finished up. He was exceptionally gifted, both in composing and singing. His death was a huge loss to the music industry.'

There was speculation that the intention was to have The Miami wagon blown up with the musicians, thereby creating the impression that they were involved in smuggling weapons and explosives. These sorts of rumours about Southern showbands, which were entirely without foundation, circulated regularly.

On 15 October, 1976, at Belfast High Court, two former members of the UDR, Thomas Raymond Crozier (25), and James Roderick McDowell (29), both of Lurgan, were sentenced to life imprisonment for their part in the massacre. At the end of a seven-day trial, Lord Justice Jones recommended that they serve not less than 35 years each. Five years later, in 1981, a third man, John James Somerville (37), of Dungannon, Co. Tyrone, was also jailed for a minimum of 35 years for the murders. Crozier and McDowell have since been released.

Stephen Travers survived his injuries and is now living in London. Des Lee emigrated to South Africa.

The attack on The Miami made no sense. Music had always transgressed all sectarian and religious divides. The band itself comprised both Catholics and Protestants. Bands from the North had huge respect in the South, and vice versa.

Speaking on the tenth anniversary of the massacre, Dickie Rock told the *Evening Herald*: 'I often wonder what they would look like today and what they be doing now. It's the type of thing that keeps coming back to you. I said at the time I would never go up North again. Of course things change.'

Up to then the showband industry had been a thirty-two-county business. According to RTE's Ronan Collins, the massacre made people in the South more aware of the whole physical border.

'It also brought home to us the whole, needless, wanton violence that was going on. Here was a totally innocent group of men annihilated for no reason at all. It caused a terrible division in the showband scene, because now you were either a Northern band or a Southern band. It also helped to bring about the demise of the whole business, which was already on the wane.'

The killings had major repercussions for The Paddy Cole Superstars. All bands stopped going to the North and this sounded the death knell for The Superstars as all their publicity was concentrated there.

'We started to play more in the South, but we didn't get the crowds. I remember going to Longford one night and the attendance would not have paid for the petrol for the wagon. It's the side of the business that people don't see.

'We pulled out for two or three months. Then came the time to decide whether to fold up altogether or go back up again. We sat down and talked it through and agreed to go back up.'

There were other setbacks. Paddy Cole was forced to leave the band temporarily for an operation in Navan hospital. He had long suffered from a disc problem in his back. 'I remember one night Mike Dalton driving me to a gig with the seat stretched fully back, as I was in extreme pain. I still had to get out and play for the night.'

'Everywhere we went people used to give Paddy some magic remedy for his back,' says Twink. 'Or he'd get the name of another bone crusher and he'd be off to see him the following Tuesday. I used to feel sorry for him because I could see the pain etched in his face. It was tough driving 200 miles or so, doing a rehearsal, followed by a break and a two-hour show beginning at midnight. There were no showers, even though you would be a walking rag of perspiration. Paddy would then get back into the car and drive the 200 miles back home.'

When Cole returned, Colm Hughes was out fronting the band with Twink. She left shortly afterwards to pursue her own solo career.

'Twink never really liked the scene even when she was doing well. She had to sing country and western numbers, which she hated, but I had no sympathy for her because you have to give the punters what they want.'

Finally, tired of the road, Twink decided to tell Cole she had had enough.

'I really hated the business, and at the risk of being a total snob, I felt it was way beneath me. They used to say I was a snobby bitch anyway, only interested in theatre and television. The only thing that got me through the business was Paddy. I also dreaded the band holidays because the boys would all go off with their wives while any girlfriends I had would have taken their two weeks during our busy time. So I had to find some kind of a holiday for myself!'

One year Twink decided to return to Vegas 'just for pig iron'.

'It had been two years since I was there, so I just sat and watched the shows. Brendan and The Big 8 were somewhere up the Strip, and not in The Stardust, where we played. One night I went to see Diana Ross and I looked at the stage and the set, the costumes and the lighting and I thought to myself: "Why did I ever leave?" It was not the band I was in that depressed me, but the situation I had to work in.

The first place we played, when we came back from holidays, was in The Starlight Ballroom in Westport. I spent all day rehearsing with the band, including a new number, *Evergreen*, which had been recorded by Barbara Streisand. The only reason Paddy let me sing it was because there is a magnificent flute solo in it (Cole once hyperventilated and fell off a stool unconscious while rehearsing it at home).

"Twink, it's too feckin' sophisticated, the punters won't understand it," he argued with me.

"I don't give a shit, Paddy," I shouted. "If I'm going to sing the rest of the crap, I need to sing some good song or I'll lose my marbles."

Cole was reluctant to let Twink perform numbers like *Evergreen* and *Pearl's a Singer* because The Superstars were competing against the ever increasing competition from country music.

'When Paddy introduced *Evergreen* the punters were perplexed. They couldn't make head nor tail of it. It wasn't a waltz or anything they could recognise. However, as soon as I started the vocal, the men were across the floor in a flash, grabbing women. As I looked down at them I said to myself: "Twink, I don't know what you are going to do for a living, but I know what you are not going to do ever again".'

The next night was even worse — the venue, a marquee in Cavan.

'That was the night the committee had me change in a small, dilapidated shed behind the marquee unless I wanted to go up to the priest's house two miles away. I changed in the shed into a one-piece white jump suit, with white boots from London, before going on to a makeshift stage.'

After the dance was over, Twink found Cole arguing with a member of the committee over the fee for the night.

' "Listen here, boss," says Paddy, "they're not three flower pots I have at home. They like to sit up and eat occasionally. Now give us the fuckin' readies, boss." And with that, the committee handed over the extra ton. "Thanks very much, boss," says Paddy, "we'll not be back."'

Back in the car there was an unusual silence for 20 miles.

'He was white-knuckled and twitching and I thought it a bad time to say I was unhappy. Eventually he turned round to me and said: "Well, Gertie, you're not saying a lot. What's the matter? Come on, out with it."

"Ah, it can wait," I pleaded.

"No, come on girl, out with it now. What's the problem?"

"Ah, there's a time and place for everything," I said.

"You can't hack it, can you?" he blurted out suddenly. "I know what you're going to tell me. You're compounding the wonderful evening I'm having. You're leaving the band?"

"Paddy, I can't take it," I whispered. "I can't take it any more. It's breaking my heart. It's not you. It's not the band. You know I love you. You know I love the boys, but I can't do this anymore".

'When I told manager Tony Loughman I was leaving, his reaction was to tell me: "No one leaves a band under my management." So I told him: "Tony, there is a first for everything. Good afternoon."

'And so I walked out, and into what I don't know. A void of nothingness for ages, but you've got to take risks. I look at people in the business who hated it, and some of them are still there. Sometimes now I pass these big empty ballrooms and, God forgive me, they remind me of Auschwitz.'

While he regretted her departure, Paddy Cole bore no grudges against Twink. 'When I went round to The Gaiety and saw how successful she was in pantos and musicals,' he says, 'I was delighted for her. She has an unbelievable talent, and is a great worker, though sometimes a bit too conscientious. She lets nobody away with anything.'

When Cole returned to the band after his illness, there was a major surprise in store for him. Colm Hughes did not want him back on stage because he felt he was too old!

'I was rocked to my heels. Effectively, there was another coup going on. I was given the charming title of "Promotions Manager", which meant nothing as Tony Loughman did all that side of the business. Being Promotions Manager meant I might roll up a few posters and send them out to various venues. I said to hell with this, and I cut clean.'

Paddy with Twink and her husband David Agnew on their wedding day. In the background is Mike Murphy.

8
A DIPLOMAT AND A DOORMAT

It's 8a.m. on a June Sunday in 1979. A major sporting occasion in the calendar of the GAA is to take place — Armagh and Monaghan are to play in the Ulster Championship in Clones.

Paddy Cole is asleep in his new home outside Castleblaney. The previous night was, as usual, busy in his pub in the centre of the town, and he did not get to bed until the small hours.

Suddenly there was a knock on the bedroom window. Hey, Paddy,' shouted his brother-in-law Sean McCarthy. 'Get to fuck out of the bed. There's murder in 'Blaney over that Armagh flag flying high over the pub.'

'What Armagh flag?' asked a bleary-eyed Cole. 'I know nothing about any Armagh flag.'

He jumped out of bed and headed for the pub on the corner of Main St. and York St., a prominent place in the town, through which thousands of Armagh supporters would pass on their way to Clones. As he drove down the street, he was astonished to see a giant Armagh flag flying high above his pub, with its pole firmly secured in the chimney.

Cole was immediately suspicious of the culprits, the McMahons, well known Armagh supporters, who frequented the pub and were good friends of Paddy's. One of the boys, Fran McMahon, now living in Chicago, played football for Armagh. At the time of the match another brother, Gerry, was painting the premises, and his ladders were in the backyard. Later it emerged that Gerry McMahon had laid several bets with fellow countymen that there would be an Armagh flag flying over Cole's pub when they drove by on their way to the match on Sunday morning.

Cole called on the help of Gene Duffy, a local lad who worked with him, and together they erected some of the McMahon ladders.

'When I got to the roof I had to crawl up along the slates to the chimney. The pole must have been at least 20 feet down the chimney because I was there for ages trying to pull it up.'

By now a crowd was gathering on the street below. When the flag finally came tumbling down and hit the street, a huge cheer went up. Soon the Armagh followers started to pass by. Gerry McMahon's jaw dropped when the flag, which he had painstakingly erected during darkness the previous night, was nowhere to be seen. He had to pay out, and substantially.

The Coles had decided to move to Castleblaney shortly after The Superstars were formed.

'We were doing most of our work in the North and I was driving up and down to Dublin needlessly. The driving was shared between Mike Dalton and myself. Sometimes we would only have to bring Twink home because she wanted to go to some dog show or other.

Paddy discussed the move with Helen and they decided that if they moved to 'Blaney, they would buy a bar there.

The manager of The Superstars Tony Loughman, lived in 'Blaney and owned a large licensed premises there, The Three Star Inn, which was on the market.

'I was trying to do a deal with him, but was frustrated by a phone strike at the time.' When he finally called to Loughman's, a local contractor, Frank Reilly, was sitting in the kitchen.

'Tony,' I said, 'I'd like to talk to you about the bar deal.'

'Oh, Paddy, I'm sorry I didn't think you were interested,' said Loughman. 'I've just sold it to Frank Reilly.'

A disappointed Cole headed down town and into Macartan Moore's pub on the corner of Main St. and York St. for a sandwich.

'While I was talking to him, didn't Mac happen to mention he was thinking of selling out and going back to America where his father-in-law, Alan Clancy, owned a number of pubs. Clancy advised me not to buy it, even though it was his son-in-law who was selling. He said it was a very tough life and I was mad to be going into it.'

Cole stayed in 'Blaney that night and the following morning surveyed Mac Moore's. He ended up buying the pub.

Paddy Cole, publican, now aged 39, had entered a new phase of his career. The pub was renamed 'Paddy Cole's Place'.

'I drove back to Dublin in a lather of sweat wondering what I was doing and what bank manager's arm I would twist. But I knew I was selling my house on Taney Road in Dublin and would have some cash.'

When selling the house, Cole called in the services of his old friend from the showband days, solicitor Eddie Masterson. The family moved to 'Blaney in 1978, and at first stayed in a house owned by Tony Loughman.

'I had got good advice never to live over a pub because I would have been tormented morning, noon and night by people looking for drink. We organised some finance — we were very ambitious — and built our own house outside the town on the Carrickmacross Road.'

There was a restaurant over the bar, and Helen Cole, a former student of Cathal Brugha St., used her skills to introduce some fresh food ideas to the people of Co. Monaghan and surrounding areas.

'When you go into business, you learn the hard way,' says Paddy. 'There were guys who I was in school with in 'Blaney who never stood in the bar. There was a lot of small town begrudgery from guys who did not come in because they hated to see anybody doing well. Having lived in Dublin and the United States, I found it difficult to come to terms with all that small town stuff. Dermot O'Brien, who later bought a bar in Ardee, concurred with me about this small-town begrudgery. Little did they know that I was up to my neck in debt.'

It took time to adapt to the ways of the crafty 'Blaney publicans.

'You had to get used to the cute men at publicans' meetings, particularly when it came to the issue of putting up the price of drink. At one meeting we all agreed to increase drink prices. The following night my customers were complaining that the price had not increased in other bars, but you soon became a cute man yourself.'

The clientele was a mixed bag.

'Every pub has its own clientele, and you do not expect guys who drink in other bars to move to your pub, but a lot of fellows did come in to support me and then go on to their own local. I could understand that, but I found it hard to accept that guys for whom I had done a few good turns would not come in.'

But there was help available from some local friendly publicans, men like John Beatty, the piano player with the Mainliners, who owned a pub in Castleblaney and Pakie 'Tarzan' Donaghy, a former boxer.

'Pakie was, for example, in the pub the night my grandmother died. I asked him what should I do. He told me to close the doors, let the people who were there finish their drinks and leave. So I bought them all a drink, and Pakie and myself sat and talked.'

But Cole ignored some of Pakie's other advice, and lived to regret it. 'If I had taken it, I would have been a better publican, unpopular at the beginning, but accepted later for what I was doing. Instead I started off like most publicans, being popular with everyone and then not so popular with the "touchers". Pakie warned me never to loan money to anybody and never let the best customer think he owns the place, or that anything he says has to be done. I didn't follow his advice. I gave out loans. I cashed cheques that bounced. When I finally sold the bar I was owed £860 in fivers and tenners. It wasn't an awful lot of money, but it just shows how it accumulates.'

Paddy approached one 'borrower' seeking the return of his 'loan.' Unknown to Paddy, the man had strong paramilitary connections.

'He told me I could do what I liked, but to be careful what I did. So I just left it.'

Cole learned the hard way that it is better for publicans not to give loans.

'The people that owed me money were the very same people who went around saying: "Paddy Cole's a miserable old bollix". You give a loan of £20 to someone, and he doesn't give it back. He doesn't come in any more, and therefore he is no longer a customer. In addition he is now bad-mouthing you around the place, so you lose on the double. I got used to it. It's the same everywhere. Publicans all over Ireland will bear that out.

'I had the best of customers in the bar. I drove them home, brought them to dances, did everything for them, and then, when the slightest thing happened in the bar when I was not around, they stopped coming in. When they left, they took three or four fellows with them. I learned an awful lot about small town bars. As one barman told Gay Byrne on the *Late Late Show,* you have to be both a diplomat and a doormat.

'Often at night time I had to sit there listening to a few guys finishing their drink even though I was anxious to finish up and go home after a hard day's work. You valued your customers so much that you put up with listening to the bullshit.'

Sunday nights were particularly busy when crowds came across the Border from South Armagh, areas like Crossmaglen, Cullyhanna, Culloville and Newtownhamilton. They expected to be allowed stay on well after closing time.

'I foolishly believed two other publicans who told me they were going to close at 11p.m. sharp on Sundays. I told my staff to stop serving. There was a lot of pressure from some of the guards to clear the place. The first and second Sunday night I stopped serving at 11p.m. on the dot. On the third Sunday night, the staff were sitting down watching television at 11p.m. The two other pubs were packed . . . and still serving.

'I fell for a lot of these things in the beginning. I knew they were having a laugh at me, and saying behind my back: "Your man Cole, he should have stuck to the music". I learned to meet fire with fire, and brought the crowds back. '

Every time somebody came into the pub they expected to meet Paddy himself. He frequently had to leave his dinner, and drive back into the pub. His sister, Carmel, came and helped out.

'Carmel had a great way with customers. If a guy with too much drink was awkward, Carmel would walk up to him and say: "Cop yourself on, you scamp you". But if I said that, the same guy would put me on my arse on the floor.'

There were embarrassing moments, too.

'I was late arriving in for a Monday night music session because I was bringing the money floats with me. I was coming through the door late, with two bags of money and instruments strung over my shoulder when this lad, with his two feet on a newly refurbished bar stool, shouted: "Howy'a Paddy?"

I looked at him and snapped: "Get your fuckin' feet off that stool fast".

'Five minutes later I saw the guy going to the toilet, on crutches. He was an invalid. I was devastated. Later I spoke to him about it, and, fair play to him, we had a laugh about it.'

It was an era when Derry City soccer team started to do well in the League of Ireland, and attracted a huge following. Everybody talked about the great Derry supporters, and how Catholics and Protestants all mingled together without any animosity. They were renowned for their discipline. Troublesome supporters were reputed to be banned from all future matches. They received very favourable publicity in the newspapers. Paddy Cole's experience was to the contrary.

'We willingly took busloads of supporters in for meals as they returned from the matches. The official supporters were first class. However, it was reported in the local paper in Derry that they had stopped in Paddy Cole's Place for a meal, and everybody arrived. These supporters turned out to be some of the roughest I have ever seen, and wrecked the pub several nights. They broke down the door at the back of the pub, and took a few kegs of beer on to the bus with them. They did the same to other pubs, including the Emyvale Inn where the barmen had to run for shelter behind the counter.

'One night even the poor boxes went missing from the counter, but others among them organised a collection to make it up and much more. It got to the stage that when Derry City were playing in Dublin or Dundalk, I closed the doors and only let the locals in. I used to dread it for a week in advance. Mostly, they fought among themselves and not with the locals. There many decent guys among them and they organised their own entertainment.'

Paddy Cole was strict in the way he ran his pub.

'The location led guys to believe they could slip across the Border, do what they liked, and then slip back again, but I followed it through. For example, one fellow smashed a window because I refused to serve him, and drove off across the Border. I took the car reg number and reported it to a local garda sergeant. He, in turn, got on to the RUC in Armagh and we traced him down until he had to come back, apologise and pay for the window.

In maintaining order in the pub, Paddy relied on local guys and friends like Aidan McMahon from Culloville and Brian Duffy from Castle-blaney. McMahon, a friend of Cole's, was a very tall hardy man, whose presence at the counter was enough to ensure there would be no trouble.

The biggest night of the week in Paddy Cole's Place was Monday, when the popular music sessions attracted crowds from far and wide. The session was always the highlight.

Paddy, who continued his interest in music, was joined by his old friend Maurice Lynch, and the guitarist from the Maurice Lynch Band, Gerry Muldoon, along with Jimmy Smyth, Freddie Ryan on trombone, Gabriel McQuillan on bass and Ronnie Duffy — now with the Mainliners — or his son Mark on drums along with Butch McNeil and Micky McCarthy who had both played with The Paddy Cole Superstars.

Everybody was welcome for the sessions which achieved national fame. RTE came and made a programme.

'They came from everywhere,' says Paddy, 'from Ballybay and Carrickmacross. Glamorous girls started to come to the sessions for a night out, and they, of course, brought the local 'terriers' in pursuit. One night I turned to my son, Pearse, and quipped: "Son, this place is like a powder keg. I can see smugglers and customs men, army officers, police officers, IRA men, INLA men, all here together. One spark and it's gone!" But it was always a happy night. Only once did a smuggler, who had too much drink taken, slag off a couple of customs officers. When I challenged him he said a few words too many. I grabbed him by the scruff of the neck and threw him out. I liked the guy, but I had to bar him.

'Gerry O'Donnell, who owns a pub in Crossmaglen, was a great friend of mine and warned me that if you bar someone, he or she must be barred for life. There was one chap from Armagh City, whom I barred because when he was drunk he used to hit people. A year later when he was off the drink completely for nine months, he came in and asked for a mineral. But I said to him: "I know you're on the straight and narrow, but I can't bend the rules for anybody."

"But I'm not drinking," pleaded the reformed customer.

"I know," I said, "but the day might come, and I hope it doesn't, when you might go back on the drink, and then you'll think you're allowed in here. So you're still barred. OK?" I didn't like having to do it, but we ran a strict operation. I took Gerry O'Donnell's advice there.'

Paddy trained many of his nephews in the business and today they are top barmen, some of them working in The Glencarn Hotel in 'Blaney.

'I taught all those guys the hard way, and I gave it to them in the neck if anything was wrong, but they are a credit now.'

The Monday night sessions provided the basic income for the week.

'On Tuesdays, Wednesday and Thursdays you could fire a canonball through the pub and hit no one.'

Old friends form the showband days also helped out with advice, like ballroom owner Brendan Mulgrew from Cookstown.

'I was planning to put Liscannor stone on the front of the pub and I discussed it with Mulgrew who had been a contractor in England. He told me to call down to Cookstown, and look at the stone on the bank on the main street. A few days later he phoned and said to me: "You needn't be coming down — she's out on the road". I asked him what in the name of God was he talking about. "The bank!" he declared. "It's out on the street — in pieces, blown up".'

But Paddy Cole found the strain of a publican's life hard going, particularly the after-hours drinking.

'Our biggest problem was trying to get fellows out. The small town begrudgery was amazing. Our pub would be packed on Monday nights, with obvious spin-offs for the other pubs and shops in town. Yet other publicans would ring the guards complaining that Cole's was packed and ask what were they going to do about it. Later I got the names of those who complained and I was amazed.'

A local man from Castleblaney, Sean McCooey, worked as a barman in Phibsboro in Dublin for Alan Clancy.

'One Sunday night I was standing at the door of the pub getting a breath of air, with still 30 or 40 people inside, when McCooey pulled up beside me for a chat. He had already locked up and driven home to 'Blaney. In 'Blaney people only went out at closing time.'

These days Paddy Cole has the height of sympathy for barmen. There's no better man for a pint than myself, but when the barman calls "Time" I'm the first to get up and go.'

One summer's night in 1986 he was standing at the door of his pub when he saw a neighbouring publican rolling a keg of beer around the corner to take in to serve customers.

'I looked at my watch. It was a quarter to one. The thought suddenly struck me that this was the way I'm going to finish up — rolling in a keg at a quarter to one in the morning to try to keep three or four fellows happy. And at that moment I made up my mind — I was getting out.'

The following evening Cole summoned a family meeting over tea. He and Helen turned to their three children, Pearse, Pat and Karen, and asked: 'Which of you is going to take over the pub when we retire?' All three laughed at their father's suggestion.

'As youngsters they had worked in the pub collecting glasses. Often when they came home from school I would pull them in behind the counter for an hour, but they might be there for three or four. Like a lot of children who grow up in pubs, they grew to hate it. They told me they would not take it over for a million pounds. So I turned to Helen and said: "I'm selling the pub".'

"I'm delighted," she replied. There was an immediate air of relief.

'You have to slave from 10.30a.m. to well after midnight — more than 15 hours a day — when you could earn as much with less hassle from two hours a night on stage,' Cole told local reporter Patsy McArdle in a interview for the *Sunday Press*.

Philip Brady who had worked for Macartan Moore and Paddy Cole, and his brother Martin, had long been talking about buying a pub. They were sons of the famous Cavan footballer of the '40's, 'The Gunner' Brady.

'After a lot of coming and going we struck a deal and the boys bought the pub. They renamed it "The Gunner Brady's" and today it's a thriving business.'

Paddy Cole was out of the pub business for good.

'I still have some great friends who came into the pub and I meet them regularly. Running the pub was the best learning experience I had during my lifetime. When we moved back to Dublin, we had notions of going back into the bar business, but I'm the happiest man in Ireland that we didn't.'

He looked at a few pubs that were for sale with Dublin publican Dessie Hynes.

'I strongly advised Paddy against buying a pub,' says Hynes. 'It's very hard for anybody who has any other talent to run a pub. A good chef will make more money without a pub. A good musician will make more money without a pub.'

Hynes concurs with Cole's view of the publican's life.

'I grew up in Longford and I know what it's like in a small town. There are publicans wooing other pubs' clients, even on Dublin's Baggot St. where there are thousands of people passing every day. One guy lets them in half an hour before opening on Sunday mornings by standing outside and letting on to be sweeping the street. That's what it's like.

'In my view there's only one way to own a pub, and that's to have it paid for. Then you can run it as you wish. You can't have a pub that belongs to the customers. It already belongs to the health authorities, the police authorities, the insurance company, the income tax man and other invisible people, all of whom would keep you awake at night if you let them.'

These days Paddy Cole enjoys a pint after a gig in The Harcourt Hotel on Sunday nights, or round at his local, Andy Ryan's pub, The Waterloo or Hynes on Baggot St. Bridge, where a large pike, which he once caught in Lake Muckno, beside Castleblaney, hangs on the wall in a glass case.

'Paddy Cole is proud that he caught that fish and likes people to see it,' says Dessie Hynes. 'Paddy is a fisherman — just like Our Lord and St Peter!'

9
DEATH DOGS THE CAPITOL

Proprietor Pat Jennings of the The Travellers Friend Hotel, Castlebar had invited Paddy Cole, now a solo musician, to do a spot with the resident hotel band.

'I arrived full of the joys of spring because Sonny Knowles had given me some advice on how to do a solo act. I met the three lads in the band and discussed the programme. I discarded a few numbers with which they were not familiar.'

Cole asked for the drummer, whom he regarded as a key player in any band. 'He's a very quiet fellow,' they told me, 'not a word out of him. And one thing about him, Paddy, he'll not drink your pint while you are playing your numbers.'

Cole walked out on stage.

'There it was, on a chair in front of me, a feckin' drum machine! I looked down at all the people sitting there that would have known me from The Capitol, The Big 8 and The Superstars, and said: "Lads, we should have worked out the tempos first".

'We opened with a fairly fast number, but the drum machine comes in: "dunk................dunk..............dunk........."

'That's far too slow, lads,' I shouted. The machine then goes: "dunk...dunk...dunk...dunk...dunk..." away flying on its own! But I had to settle for it. The boys were fine, but that drum machine put years on me that night. To this day, if I have any bad nights I keep thinking of that drum machine on the chair beside me in Castlebar, and I say to myself: "Things are not that bad."'

Since he had left The Superstars and bought the pub in Castleblaney, Paddy Cole had been out of the music scene other than for the Monday night sessions.

Shortly before he sold the pub, his old friend Twink, and her husband David Agnew, rang and invited himself and Helen to a meal in Clontarf Castle. The occasion turned out to be an invite to do a spot on her cabaret show in the Castle. It was a new departure for Cole.

'I was trembling in my shoes. Never before had I gone out on my own with just a three-piece band, well not since the days of Sally and Kevin McKenna anyway.

'That's when I learned what showbusiness is all about. It's not about getting a standing ovation in the Capitol Showband reunion in the Braemor Rooms when they would have cheered even if we played *Ba Ba Black Sheep*. Showbusiness is about going out on your own and trying to entertain people while they are eating. I once did a guest spot on my own in the Country Club in Portmarnock, when Willy Morris owned it. The Mersey Beats who were a huge attraction in Liverpool came over but drew a very small crowd. It fell to me to entertain the customers while they were having a meal. They didn't even want to leave down their knife and fork to clap.

'I got a lot of experience that I thought I already had. I got a completely fresh look at the business. This was a new challenge, and I decided to take it. In other bands the only reason I often sang was because I was the only one who knew the words. Now I had to sing for a living. I worked with Susan McCann in Clontarf Castle, Earl Gill, Cathy Nugent, Tina, Helen Jordan, Ann Bushnell and many others in the cabaret scene.'

Paddy Cole is proud of his comeback to the music business. Up to that time he had never been a front man, and few would have known of him other than as a sax player. Now all that changed.

'I tried to entertain people as best I could. If they didn't appreciate me, I simply smiled and said: "Well, movin' right along."

'Tom Dunphy used to tell me that when Lonnie Donegan went to Vegas doing his skiffle songs, people there could not understand him because of his cockney accent. They sat there with puzzled looks on their faces and he got bad reaction. It got to the stage when Lonnie used to say: "Good evening Opposition, here's another one you won't like . . . ." I used to think of Lonnie some nights.'

'Any true entertainer who has paid his or her dues has done those gigs. That's where the term comes from. The survivors in the business, like Dickie Rock, Joe Dolan, Linda Martin and Red Hurley have all paid their dues. Sonny Knowles went all over the country on his own with only a button accordion to back him sometimes, but he did it.

'Brush Shields told me that there is nothing you can do to make an audience change their mind about you. You do your act and that's it.'

Life as a solo entertainer can be tough and lonely.

'Paddy Reilly was once sitting in Fitzpatrick's Hotel in New York when U2 came in and joined him for a cup of coffee. Paddy got up, lifted his guitar and threw an overnight bag over his shoulder. He said he was catching a plane to Boston.

"But Paddy," inquired Bono, "where is your equipment?"

"That's it," replied Reilly, pointing to the single guitar.

U2 had six articulated trucks of equipment with them on tour.

But I admire guys like Paddy Reilly and Mick Hanley. Old troubadours. Have guitar, will travel.

'I also have great admiration for Dermot O'Brien, who was in the pub business in Ardee. When that did not work out, he and his wife Rosemary went to the States where he took out his accordion. He became a huge name and one of the major draws on the American–Irish circuit. He is also now resident in Jury's Dublin Summer Cabaret.'

In early 1984 Paddy Cole got a phone call in Castleblaney from his former Capitol Showband colleague Des Kelly, now living in Galway. Kelly had been asked by local priest, Fr Sean Foy, a friend of The Capitol in their heyday, to try to put the band together again for a function in his Salthill bar, The Castle, to raise funds for a church at Tireallan, then a new parish on the Headford Road. Down the road from The Castle was Salthill's Seapoint Ballroom, where The Capitol had attracted huge crowds for many years.

By now a 'Ballroom of Romance', that night it was filled with theatre-goers attending the Druid presentation of "Famine". The support band to The Capitol in The Castle was a group called Level Crossing. Some of its members had not even been born when the Capitol was packing them into the Seapoint.

Eamonn Monahan, Jimmy Hogan, Paul Sweeney, and Paddy Cole of the original Capitol drove down from Dublin to the Galway function. Butch Moore was unable to make it as he was presenting a regular radio show in Washington at the time.

Word had spread that The Capitol was going to be reunited, and The Castle was packed. Ronnie Drew and Phil Coulter were just two of the celebrities who arrived. Some members of the band had not set eyes on each other since they broke up some 15 years earlier. However, a few short hours of rehearsals brought back the old magic that had put them to the top in the 1960s. The function received major coverage in the national daily newspapers.

'They may not have sported the traditional blue jackets and white trousers of yesteryear, but there was no doubting the authentic flavour of the music,' wrote reporter John Walshe in the *Irish Independent*.

Walshe reported that it was nostalgia all the way for the Valentine's night lovers as the band rang out old favourites like *The Streets of Baltimore* and *The Black Velvet Band*.

Trombone player Don Long, who flew over from Manchester for the event, belted out *Angeline* with all his old gusto while pianist Eamonn Monahan brought back memories with his version of *Big Bad John*. Guitarist Jimmy Hogan brought back memories, too, with his version of *Mise Eire*. During the night Paddy Cole was presented with a silver disc by Brendan Harvey of K-Tel for sales of his record, *Music Man*. The night sparked off rumours of further reunions. A meeting was called in Dublin to tease out the idea.

'We met in a restaurant where Eamonn Monahan used to play the piano at night time. Des Kelly arrived with a young fellow who was running his pub entertainment and proposed he manage the tour. I put my neck on the block, and said: "If we are going to do this, then let's do it properly. I turned to the young lad and said: "If we were going to do a gig in Cork, how would you go about it?" He mentioned some promoter in Galway he would phone for advice.

'I said that, with all due respect, it was the person he was phoning we should have managing the tour. The meeting ended in disarray because I recommended Tony Loughman of Top Rank Promotions, who would be guaranteed to do a professional job. We agreed to differ, shook hands and I headed back to the pub in Castleblaney.'

Meanwhile, the rest of the group headed to Paul Sweeney's Dublin home to watch a video of the night in Salthill, which Des Kelly had brought with him. 'Later that night Johnny Kelly phoned me from Paul Sweeney's house to say they had talked again and agreed the tour should be organised professionally. He said a few of them wanted me to be the band leader. Des Kelly, who had been the leader of The Capitol, had no crib about it.'

Cole approached Tony Loughman, who strongly approved of a reunion tour and set about booking venues around the country. Many of them were run in conjunction with fund-raising projects, including the roofing of Mount Argus in Dublin, a project promoted by Fr Brian D'Arcy.

Advance publicity was arranged along with brochures, T-shirts, towels and souvenir programmes. The tour opened in the Braemor Rooms in Churchtown and was a sell-out before it was even advertised.

Paddy with Phil Coulter on the day he was presented with a silver disc by K-Tel for sales of his album Music Man. The disc hangs on the wall of the Paddy Cole bar in Blarney Park Hotel.

'It was the first time I saw ads on the back of *The Irish Times* where people were looking for tickets, as for a major international match,' says Cole. 'It became the show to go to.'

Rehearsals were inadequate, due to the fact that Butch Moore and Don Long were late arriving, and the general confusion of trying to get a band together after 15 years.

When the band came on stage, dressed in their traditional blue jackets and white slacks, they were given a standing ovation before they played a note.

'I looked down and the first person I saw standing up was Joe Cuddy who was in the centre of the room with a party of 20. I also saw Joe Dolan among other familiar faces. Muriel Quinn, the proprietor, was in a sweat about the show, but we had music parts planted all over the stage so that we could read the unfamiliar bits. She gave us the thumbs up from the floor, too.'

The show went better than the musicians expected. And the audience loved it. 'Died-in-the-wool musicians might have wondered what it was all about, but people still come up to me and say it was the best show they were ever at. Some of the guys had put on a few stone weight, others — including myself — had lost our hair. Out in the car park the array of cars was unbelievable — Jaguars, Mercedes, BMWs, all former fans of the band who had done well in life. It was probably the best week the Braemor Rooms ever had.'

The show stayed in the Braemor Rooms for one week, and then went on a national tour. Everywhere the reaction was the same. Prolonged standing ovations from the former fans and from some younger music enthusiasts as well.

The schedule was hectic. The band tried to live as they had 15 years before. 'We were up drinking all night with old friends around the country, and then getting up early to play golf in the morning.'

That soon took its toll.

'We played two gigs in Donegal town. After the first, some of the lads from The Clipper Carlton, including Micky O'Hanlon and

Terry Logue, came to see the show and we all ended up in a long night session. As usual the next morning we were up playing golf. Before the second show, Sean 'The Spoofer' Jordan — who was back as road manager — was supposed to have the band in the hall well in advance. Suddenly a panic-stricken Tony Loughman arrived at the hotel to see what was wrong. Not alone were all the members asleep, but The Spoofer, who was supposed to be in charge, was himself asleep.'

Members of The Capitol Showband in Mullingar during their reunion in 1984 with lifelong fan, Prandy Duffy. Back row: (front left) Paddy Cole, Don Long, Eamonn Monahan, Jimmy Hogan, Paul Sweeney, Butch Moore. Front row: Johnny Kelly, Prandy Duffy and Des Kelly.

The following day the band passed through Castleblaney *en route* to Dundalk, and stopped for a meal in Paddy Cole's Place. Within minutes Paul Sweeney was stretched out on the floor asleep. Guitarist Jimmy Hogan was feeling unwell too, and refused to have any food.

'Jimmy, when are you going to eat something?' asked an anxious Cole.

'About next Saturday,' replied the badly hung-over Hogan.

Loughman imposed a new reign of discipline. The late night drinking sessions were banned, and the golf was restricted. By the time the tour ended some dissension had set in.

'Des Kelly probably felt he should have been the band leader, and a few other niggeldy things happened.'

But there were demands for more tours. Muriel Quinn wanted The Capitol back in the Braemor Rooms. Ann D'Arcy wanted them in Clontarf Castle. A second tour was organised.

'Des Kelly pulled out and then resented the fact that we did the tour without him. His brother Johnny also pulled out because he was in bad health. Bram McCarthy could not play in any of the tours because he had a heart condition.

Then tragedy struck.

The reformed Capitol, albeit without three members, were waiting to go on stage in the Braemor Rooms when there was a telephone message to say that former drummer, Johnny Kelly, had died in London. The band was devastated, but pressed ahead with the show and only announced the death of their former colleague before leaving the stage.

There was more bad news on the way. The following night the band members were discussing the travel arrangements to Johnny Kelly's funeral over coffee when trombonist Don Long walked in to deliver another bombshell.

'You're not going to believe this, ' he announced, 'but Bram McCarthy has just died.' McCarthy, who had been ill for some time had collapsed and died in a Dublin supermarket.

The death of two members of the original Capitol Showband within 24 hours of each other was hard to take. There was another showbusiness death the same day, that of Hugo Quinn, trumpeter with The Clipper Carlton.

The band members went to Galway to attend Johnny Kelly's funeral, and then to Tallaght for the removal of Bram McCarthy. Don Long organised a New Orleans-style burial. 'We played some blues numbers in the church, and people including comedian Al Banim, who had worked with The Capitol in the Braemor Rooms, and Sonny Knowles, wept openly. Later in the graveyard we played *When the Saints Come Marching In*. Every time I pass the new Tallaght Shopping Complex I think of Bram McCarthy as he is buried in the graveyard close by. Sometimes it's still hard to believe that both Bram and Johnny are dead.'

There were no more reunions of The Capitol Showband, although Butch Moore appeared with The Paddy Cole Superstars in Clontarf Castle.

'I used to admire the way Butch never took a drink until the show was over until I discovered that as soon as I was out on the stage, and he was on his own, a waiter arrived into his dressing room with two large brandies.'

'Butch made a holiday of it and stayed at The Harcourt Hotel. He never changed one bit and cannot say "No" to anybody. So I had to move into The Harcourt myself to protect him from people buying drink for him.'

'Today Butch and his wife, Maeve Mulvaney, continue to do the circuit in the US. I wish him the very best; he's one of nature's gentlemen!'

10
HELEN COOKS UP A ROMANCE

February, 1965. Paddy Cole and his wife of just ten days, Helen Hehir, are asleep in their hotel bedroom in The Regent Palace Hotel in London.

The couple had enjoyed only a few days honeymoon in Torremolinos when a call came through from the manager of the Capitol, Jim Doherty, summoning Paddy home to appear on the Eamon Andrews TV show in London.

The Coles arranged their flight back and were booked into The Regent Palace. They checked in late and went to bed.

Early the next morning the telephone rang, and a stern male voice announced: "Good morning, Mr Cole, this is reception here. I must ask you to leave the hotel at once."

"What?" asked a sleepy Cole.

"I must ask you to vacate your room at once, sir."

"Listen here to me, you. I'm booked in here for three days and I'm staying right here."

"Sir, it has been brought to our attention that you have a young lady with you in the room that you should not have."

"Excuse me. That is my WIFE."

"That's not the way we heard it, sir."

"Now listen here to me, you. . . . '

With that, a familiar Donegal voice came on the line: 'How y'a Paddy? How's it going, scout?'

A friend of his, Ignatius Murray — now owner of Iggie's bar in Kinscasslagh, Co. Donegal, and a neighbour of Daniel O'Donnell's — was a manager in the hotel, and had persuaded one of his colleagues to make the hoax call.

The Capitol duly appeared on the Eamon Andrews Show. Also appearing as a guest was Rolling Stones manager, Andrew Oldam, who told his host he could pick out anyone in the audience and name their profession.

The cameras zoomed in on the audience and focused on the newly married Helen Cole. Her husband, who was waiting in the wings to play, blushed deeply when he saw his new wife on the monitor.

'What about this lady here, Andrew?' asked Eamon Andrews.

'Hmmm.....I'd say she could be a blues singer in a nightclub, singing songs like *A Good Man is Hard to Find*,' Oldam guessed.

Andrews asked the lady who she was.

'She said "Helen Cole", which sounded strange to me because we had only been married ten days.

'Are you a singer?' asked Andrews.

'No, I'm a housewife.'

'I don't know how she came up with "housewife",' her husband recalls. 'The whole thing threw me so much I nearly fluffed my notes.'

The following morning the band went to Heathrow Airport to catch a flight home to Dublin. Recognising her face from the show, people came up to Helen and congratulated her on her TV appearance. "Oh, Mrs Cole, you were very good last night," they said.

'Nobody recognised the band,' says Paddy. 'Butch was very deflated. Eamon Monahan rang his wife in Dublin to enquire how the show had gone. 'Oh, Helen Cole was brilliant!' she replied.

Paddy Cole's first meeting with Helen Hehir from Dromcollogher, Co. Limerick, happened by chance in a ballroom in Newcastlewest in the summer of 1962.

'I was playing with The Capitol in The Olympic Ballroom in Newcastlewest when I saw this particular girl talking to a group of people, including one lad I knew who worked in a bank in Castleblaney. She told me she was going to college in Dublin and that was the end of it. I told her if she ever saw us playing nearby to be sure and drop in.'

Some weeks later Paddy Cole and drummer Johnny Kelly were driving along Dublin's Westmoreland St. in a Volkswagen beetle when Cole spotted the girl whom he he had met in Newcastlewest on the street with a friend, Phena O'Boyle.

'Hey, Johnny, there's the good-looking girl from Limerick. Pull in fast,' said an excited Cole. Kelly drew up by the pavement and Cole sprang out.

'Hey, do you remember me?' he asked excitedly.

'Hmm . . . you're the guy from The Capitol Showband. I remember you all right,' she replied.

Cole pressed her for a date and she agreed to the following Wednesday at 8p.m. 'Helen was staying in a hostel on Mountjoy Square and as I was coming from Castleblaney I was late for the date. I took a chance and rang the bell at a quarter to ten. The woman who answered said Helen had been waiting at 8pm but had gone to bed. I was asking her to tell Helen that I had called when she came down the stairs. Off we went.'

Helen Hehir was then a domestic economy student at Dublin's Cathal Brugha Street. Her parents were natives of the Currafin area of Co. Clare and the former RTE broadcaster, Michael O'Hehir, is a cousin of her late father. The family moved to Dromcollogher when her father was appointed a garda sergeant there.

The idea of her marrying a member of a showband was not initially well received by Helen's parents. He father was under the impression that Paddy Cole belonged to a circus.

'I felt Paddy was for me, but my parents were a bit concerned. It took them quite a while to come round to my way of thinking.'

There were some 'hiccups' along the route to the altar, but the couple were eventually married in Drumcondra in February 1965.

While in Cathal Brugha Street, Helen and her friend, Phena O'Boyle — later a fish cookery expert with BIM — worked as students in the restaurant in the Zoological Gardens. After qualifying, Helen transferred to the Bank of Ireland on College Green, where she ran the restaurant.

Following her marriage, she switched again, working with Guinness Group Sales to encourage publicans to introduce food for their customers.

'Up to then, a pub was very much just a meeting place for men. But Al Byrne (brother to Gay) and Justin Collins (an uncle of RTE presenter Ronan) set up courses for publicans and approached Cathal Brugha St. to nominate someone to give publicans some basic lessons in the preparation of food.

Dublin publican Dessie Hynes remembers a cousin, publican Phil Meagher, bringing him to one such course run by Guinness Group Sales in The Cherry Tree pub in Walkinstown.

'We had a number of different speakers,' Hynes recalls. 'Brian Mulcahy gave us talks on finance, on the management of money, how to borrow it and how to spend it wisely. The accounts system he gave us was very good. Helen Cole gave us talks on how to prepare pub food, chicken salads, ham salads, all sorts of salads, and how to present it attractively. I used to chat her up privately to find out how much money I could make out of this food business.'

Helen tried to teach publicans not to use everything out of a can or a packet. 'I showed them how to do basic things, and to do them well. In England husband and wife teams were running pubs and doing food, but that had not taken off in Ireland. Some knew very little, if anything, about food. One guy asked where he could possibly get parsley in a remote place like Westport. I told him that people regularly grew it in their back gardens. I taught them how to make home-made soup and stock-pots. We had great fun.'

Helen Cole ran the course for a few years until the family moved to Vegas with The Big 8, when she passed it over to a friend.

In their early married life the Coles went out together on Paddy's night off, normally Monday. They went regularly to The Old Stand bar on Exchequer Street, where the wives gathered in one corner while the men discussed sport at the bar.

One Christmas Eve, Paddy met the late Luke Kelly in The Old Stand for a drink. 'The two of us got well pissed, and of course had not bought our wives any present. It was well after closing time for the shops but we went over and knocked at the door of Brown Thomas. One of the girls, who was setting up for the after-Christmas sale, recognised Luke and let us in. We bought two shoulder handbags and much to our delight, at the sale price. Back over with us to The Old Stand, where we drank on and went home at closing time, minus the two handbags!'

Living in Vegas with a very young family was a new experience for Helen Cole. And at first she was a little naive as to the ways of the city. 'We were walking through Caesar's Palace one day,' says Paddy, 'when this very leggy blonde came up beside me and was very friendly. Helen assumed she was connected in some way with showbusiness and chatted away merrily to her. Eventually I got the message to Helen that this 'showbiz' person was a hooker who was trying to entice me upstairs! The exchanging of pleasantries came to an abrupt halt!'

Their next door neighbour was Paul Anka's father, Andy Anka. 'I remember our two boys, Pearse and Pat, going to parties there and coming home complaining that they had been served only root beer and pizzas instead of orange, coke and crisps, like at home in Ireland. It was a very different culture.'

The Cole's apartment was just off the Strip in downtown Vegas.

'We had some very good friends, many of them who had nothing to do with showbusiness,' says Helen. 'For example, we were friendly with some people from the FBI that we met through the Church.'

Life at the beginning was stimulating. Paddy Cole brought his wife to see live performances of Frank Sinatra, Elvis Presley and many others.

'I certainly enjoyed the spectacular shows and the very good food.'

But she also had more serious interests.

While Paddy was doing his shows with The Big 8 in the Stardust Hotel, Helen, an avid reader went to the library and read the works of the Nobel Literature Prize winner, Pearl S. Buck, whose father was a Chinese missionary.

'I remember often sitting in the shade of trees, reading, when I was able to identify with the loneliness of those away from home.'

The Cole's eldest son, Pearse, went to the local school, where a son of former heavyweight champion, Sonny Liston, was also a student. Drugs were always in the background and a constant worry for parents.

'I did the school run with Stella Bowyer and Maura Dunphy. When I went to parent/teacher meetings I was warned not to be late in picking up the children. So I made sure I was sitting outside the school when the class finished.'

Many years later, when playing in Killarney one summer, a middle-aged woman walked up to Paddy Cole, as he finished a number, and told him she had taught his son many years before in Vegas.

'What's he doing now?' she inquired.

'I've no idea,' replied Paddy, 'but he's doing a Master's degree in physics, and he seems to be doing all right.'

There was a natural affinity between the wives of the members of The Big 8. In the afternoons the wives, along with Twink, gathered by the swimming pool to relax. A local American doctor, Dick Allen, became a close friend of the band, as well as looking after their medical needs.

On St Patrick's Day the group introduced the first Irish parade in Las Vegas.

'We all dressed up in green,' says Helen. 'The locals thought we were all mad. For us, summer began around St Patrick's Day. But summer never "arrives" in Vegas as it is sun all year round. The roses bloomed continually, but there were no daffodils. How could you live without daffodils?'

For the Coles the family unit was all important.

'The people there did not have the commitment to the family that we had. Paddy himself came from a very large family, and they are all still very close. They keep in regular contact. When kids grew up there, they took out loans and moved out of the family home. We found those features disturbing!'

The constant reports of horrific violence also worried Helen Cole.

'I always bought the local papers on the way home from picking up the children in school, and I would read about the terrible violence here or there. Stella Bowyer once said to me: "One of the secrets of living here is not to read the papers."'

But Helen Cole insisted on reading the local papers, plus the Irish papers which arrived by post every Thursday. She was also struck by the insularity of the American way of life.

'I would tell someone about a happening in Paris or London, and they used to just look at me. They were just not interested in European or general news at all. We were always concerned about what was going on elsewhere. That I found difficult to understand.'

Every summer, when The Big 8 came home to Ireland, the Coles headed for a family holiday in Lahinch, Co. Clare. There close friends would come to visit. 'We used to walk the beach every day and I felt I had got my fix for the next year.'

By 1973 the Coles had decided to leave Vegas.

'Mentally, the way Paddy is built he would not be able to do that type of routine show continuously. He was more innovative than that. Jazz is his first passion, I'm only his second,' she jokes.

Back in Dublin, the family — which now included Pearse, born in '67; Pat, born in '70; and Karen in '72 — settled back into their old home on Dublin's Taney Road. The boys attended St Mary's School in Rathmines, while Karen went to Mt Anville.

By 1978 Paddy Cole had bought a pub in his native Castleblaney and Helen Cole suddenly found herself drawing on her old skills and running the restaurant upstairs. It served up to 100 lunches to locals, and the passing trade every day.

'I was always experimenting with food and so I filled the freezer with items like prawns, scallops and duck, but nobody ate them. I tried to vary the menu.'

One day after a customer had a fillet of plaice for main course, Helen offered him a desert.

'That's OK, Ma'm,' he said. "I've already had one.'

'Gosh, that's odd,' said Helen, 'I don't remember serving any.'

The customer had eaten the dish of tartar sauce served with the plaice, believing it to be a desert!'

Living in Co. Monaghan was not entirely new to Helen Cole. As a girl she had been a boarder with the Louis nuns in Monaghan town, and knew some of the women who were now married locally. A keen golfer, Helen joined Castleblaney Golf Club and was subsequently elected lady captain.

'I made some very good friends through golf there, and I still keep up the contact with them,' she says.

Meanwhile, the three Cole children were adapting to their new school, a typically rural, two-teacher building in Annalitten outside Castleblaney.

One day a former teacher from Rathmines, Paul Mac Murchú, who was a native of Monaghan, called to enquire how the boys were settling in. Helen expressed some concern about some of the 'unique' grammar used by pupils in the school.

'Helen,' said Mac Murchú, 'this is the only place in Western Europe where Shakespearean English is still spoken!'

On their first day in school, Helen Cole dressed up her two sons in smart new uniforms and sent them off. When they came home

Pearse declared he was not wearing a tie any more. Boys in his class had told him he was 'very posh'!

Another day the teacher Mrs McCole asked the class the correct name for a group of trees.

'A forest,' volunteered Pearse Cole.

'A wood,' said another.

Then local lad, Owen Donaghy stood up. 'A group of trees together is "a lock of trees", he declared.

'Having a rural background is something people don't really appreciate,' says Helen Cole. It's jewel in the crown. There is a microcosm of life in a small country town.'

Helen was not disappointed when her husband decided he had enough of pub life. 'I had no regrets in pulling out. We realised it was time to go. Pub life robs you of a lot of time as the hours are very long.'

The pub life made heavy demands on the children, two of whom went to boarding school in St MacCartan's in Monaghan, where they were actively involved in sports and school shows. Young Pat Cole showed something of his father's skills when he played the part of Joseph in the school's production of Joseph and His Amazing Technicolour Dreamcoat.

But living close to the Border also had its traumas. While driving from Castleblaney to Dundalk to collect supplies for the pub, Paddy and Helen were stopped by the IRA in Culloville.

"Provisional IRA, South Armagh. What is your name and where are you going?" one heavily armed gunman asked Helen, who was driving.

Helen Cole froze with fright. 'She couldn't speak and didn't answer their questions,' says Paddy. 'It was a very foggy day and I was afraid that if a British army patrol came along, they would be on top of them before they could see them. I quickly opened the window and shouted at the guy with a machine gun on the hedge: "Paddy Cole, going to Dundalk". The fellow recognised me and shouted: "It's Paddy Cole, let him on". They were involved in a show of strength, but were all very nervous. One guy warned us: "If anybody stops you up the road, you saw nothing. OK?"'

Helen Cole suddenly found her voice. 'Oh, I saw nothing,' she declared. Helen was so nervous she refused to go home by Culloville and insisted on taking the much longer route via Carrickmacross.

Back in Dublin, the Coles were on the look-out for a new home. They called to see an old neighbour on Taney Road, where they had lived.

'My God, said Paddy, 'look at that garden. The new owner has really improved it since we sold out.'

'That's amazing,' replied an alarmed Helen, 'we lived four doors further down!'

An old friend from Monaghan, Mick Sherry, drew their attention to a house in the Wellington Place area, which was up for sale. The Coles liked it and bought it. Ironically, it had been owned by a Mrs Cole, who had grown up in Co. Limerick.

By now the children were pursuing their own careers. Having graduated with a science degree from Trinity College, Pearse Cole completed his Masters in Physics at University College Cork. He joined the Kentz Group and has worked on the Olympic village in Barcelona, among other projects. He is currently working in Kuwait.

Pat studied Computer Science and German, also at Trinity, and followed with a Master's degree. He is currently based in Boston, where he works for Cambridge Technologies.

Karen studied Hotel Management in Shannon College and now works for the Hilton Group in the United States. Paddy is very proud of his children's achievements.

All three have dabbled in music, with Karen once playing clarinet with her father on the *I Live Here* RTE show. According to their mother, the family did not show the same dedication to music, as Paddy.

Wives are often given the toughest roles in showbusiness.

The Cole family at Pearse's conferring in Trinity College. From left: Pat, Helen, Pearse, Paddy and Karen.

'It's not been an easy life,' says Helen. 'But you have to make a commitment. We have a lot of common interests and we work hard at making the good times very good. Paddy is an extraordinary man. He has this driving force. No matter what obstacles are thrown in his way, he always adopts a positive attitude.

The best compliment she has heard paid to him came from a black jazz musician in New Orleans, where whites are not generally regarded as top class. 'Hey buddy,' said the black jazz man, 'for a white guy you play real good. You could have been a black man!'

11
JAZZING IT UP WITH DIZZY GILLESPIE

Sunday 2 July, 1995. The Harcourt Hotel, Dublin, home to George Bernard Shaw 121 years ago. Paddy Cole enters the large bar, his sax case slung over his right arm. He is carrying other instruments in two hand cases.

Cole greets people as he moves about, preparing for the night's gig, due to begin at nine o'clock. He appears to know everyone. In the words of *Sunday Independent* columnist Declan Lynch: "There are crusty ancients in the higher echelons of Fianna Fáil's political machine who don't know as many people as Paddy does".

It's been a hard day for Paddy Cole and his regular band. Earlier they had played a long session in the VIP tent at the Budweiser Derby at the Curragh, the highlight of the Irish racing calendar. Derby Day is now a regular date in the Cole diary.

His band that night contained some of the finest musicians around. Jimmy Hogan, a former colleague in The Capitol Showband, on guitar and banjo; Neilus McKenna, a former colleague in The Maurice Lynch band, who later played with the Altaonaires, on trumpet; Jack Bayle, a former member of The Mick Delahunty Orchestra and himself a big band leader and arranger, on trombone; Reggie Lloyd, who played with Dermot

O'Brien, on double-bass; and Johnny Christopher, who played with The Viscounts and is also a well-known singer and backing vocalist, on drums.

Some years ago when the wearing of toupees first became popular. Christopher took a part-time job as a salesman. One of his first customers was a Wicklow farmer who was slow to agree a price.

On his third visit the farmer's wife went out to the back door and yelled: 'Johnny, the man from the wiggery is here to see you!'

Christopher had had enough. Having already lost his commission on petrol to and from the farm, he abandoned the sale.

Over the years his musicians have included Peter Brady, Dessie Reynolds and RTE's Ronan Collins on drums, Michael Inight and Peter O'Brien on piano, Barry Closkey, Gerry O'Connor and Phil Cole (no relation) on clarinet and saxophone, Neville Lloyd on double-bass, Victor Proms on trombone and Paul Sweeney on trumpet.

Ronan Collins, his first drummer proved less enthusiastic than Paddy Cole required, and he got the sack!

'I went away on holiday for three weeks and when I came back Paddy had fired me,' he recalls. 'I had been replaced. I walked up to him and said: "Paddy, you fired me".

"Now hold on a second, Ronan," he says, "you told me you weren't happy doing the gig, and I got Dessie Reynolds to stand in. So he's going to stay now."

"So I'm still fired," I insisted.

"You can call it what you feckin' like, but you're not playing tonight," Paddy replied. There was no falling out about it, and in a way I was relieved as I was working in RTE at the time. My heart was not in it like his.'

Paddy Cole has been playing the Harcourt Street gig on Sunday nights for over eight years. The gig is a hallmark on Dublin Sunday nights for jazz fans, and a regular meeting point for musicians.

It now attracts large audiences, but had a very modest beginning. Eight years ago Twink and Mike Murphy were co-hosts in a charity function at The Harcourt. Twink asked Paddy, then living in Castleblaney, to put a band together for the night, and he obliged.

A few weeks later, hotel manager Jimmy Kelly rang Paddy to say he was considering doing a regular Sunday night jazz session. He asked Paddy to put a group together.

'I gave no commitment, but promised to go up and have a look at the venue. I drove up one Sunday, collected my friends Mick Sherry and Martin McArdle, both Monaghan men, and went round to The Harcourt.'

The scene that greeted them was not encouraging, a jazz group playing to an audience of four people.

'The band were typical jazz pseudos, standing on the stage with their backs to the people. This was supposed to be super-cool. In reality they were playing for themselves. To me this sort of behaviour by musicians is a load of bullshit. Louis Armstrong was the greatest jazz player, but he was also a superb entertainer and showman. There is no point in having a Jaguar in the driveway if it doesn't go.'

Cole agreed to give the jazz night a try but on condition that the proprietor, Brian McGill, agreed to stick by it for a minimum of two months.

'Brian McGill stuck by it through thick and thin, and the gig is now running for over eight years. Not only does The Harcourt have jazz, but there's music there each night of the week where the very popular entertainments manageress, Mary Cashin, has made it a major centre for gigs. It's now a meeting place for many musicians, who also stay in the hotel when in town.'

The jazz night has a regular clientele, including visitors from all over Europe and the United States who drop in year after year.

It is a rendezvous, too, for old showband hands like Maxi Muldoon, the former manager of The Clipper Carlton, former Royal Showband pianist Gerry Cullen, former impresario Jim

Hand, former Drifters drummer, Sid Aughey, Eamon Keane of The Indians, Dundalk band leader Owen Kelly, Derek Dean and Billy Brown from The Freshmen, Brian Carr from The Royal Blues, who all regularly drop in on Sunday nights.

'To hear Paddy play traditional New Orleans jazz in The Harcourt on Sunday nights, and to savour the atmosphere, is wonderful,' says Gerry Cullen.

Ronan Collins attributes the success of the night and Paddy Cole's band to their type of music and Cole's personality.

'If Paddy was to play what we call "serious jazz" he would become very bored with it. He can play it very well, but Paddy is a showman and that's what he's good at."

Paddy Cole's interest in jazz dates back to his earliest days in Castleblaney.

'I started off on the saxophone but my father had a clarinet hanging up on a nail in the bedroom, so that I couldn't get at it. But I managed to get it down and I used to practise on it when I was supposed to be learning the saxophone.'

His first introduction to jazz records was through a friend, Frank D'Arcy, from Blackrock outside Dundalk.

'Frank gave me the loan of records of players like George Lewis and Bunk Johnson. They were old-style players who never got much recognition. They were in their later years when somebody got the idea of making a recording. Bunk Johnson was a chicken farmer.

'Furthermore, many of these American jazz musicians were not allowed into good studios because they were black, and on one of Frank's records you could hear car horns blowing because the recording was made in an ordinary room on the side of the street.'

Another friend, Vincent McBrierty, now Professor of Physics in Trinity College, and who plays classical clarinet, also introduced him to jazz records which he bought in England.

'I first met him when he was a student in Queen's in Belfast when he came to our gigs. He had a great collection of jazz records and I often sneaked round to his house afterwards just to hear some of them. We are still the best of friends.'

Cole quickly developed a keen interest in New Orleans-type jazz. A sax player in The Maurice Lynch Band, Peter Hickey, alerted him to a 15-minute jazz weekly programme on Radio Luxembourg featuring Acker Bilk. 'I could not even pronounce the guy's name, but I started listening to it and thought it was fantastic. I admired his tone, and one of the greatest compliments I ever heard paid to him was many years later by an American DJ, who kept referring to the "soprano sax". Acker Bilk could create such a fat sound on the clarinet, the DJ thought it was a soprano sax.'

In The Maurice Lynch Band Paddy Cole got the opportunity to play some Dixieland jazz at the beginning of each night, with Maurice on trumpet and Gerry Duffy on trombone. They played some of the standard numbers, including *Bill Bailey, Won't You Please Come Home* and *When the Saints Come Marching In,* which was the band's signature tune.

'I will always remember one of the most embarrassing nights I ever had was with Maurice Lynch in Dungannon. Some of the guys from The Clipper Carlton, including Micky O'Hanlon and Terry Logue, came in and Maurice decided to allow me try a piece I had been practising for months, *Alexander's Ragtime Band*. I had it in a different key from the rest of the lads and off we went like a cats' concert. After the dance I stayed in the background, embarrassed, and I heard O'Hanlon telling Maurice in a humorous sort of way: "Be sure and keep that young Cole fellow out front". I felt mortified, but it made we want to practice harder.'

Cole continued to collect both modern and traditional jazz records. When on tour with The Maurice Lynch Band he regularly visited the Hundred Club on Oxford Street.

'There I saw artists like Terry Lightfoot, Sandy Browne, Acker Bilk and Ken Collier. The English bands had a major influence on us then because we could go and see them live. Some of them came over here on tour. I remember going along to see Harry Gold and his Pieces of Eight and being proud as punch to watch Joe McIntyre from Derry play trumpet with him.

'Joe was great character, a terrific musician and very much loved in the business. He died young and was a great loss. The jazz scene is still very healthy in England and Scotland, whereas a band would not survive here just playing jazz alone. Louis Stewart, one of our best guitarists and top jazz musicians, who is recognised internationally, when once asked what he would do if he won the Lotto, replied that he would continue playing jazz until he lost it again!'

Later, with The Capitol Showband, there were further opportunities for playing jazz when the night opened with an hour of Dixieland numbers featuring Paul Sweeney on trumpet, Don Long on trombone and Paddy Cole on clarinet.

Most of the bands from the North, notably Johnny Quigley, The Melotones, Dave Glover, Gay McIntyre and Jimmy Compton were all superb jazz musicians. All of them influenced and impressed Paddy Cole.

In New York The Capitol Showband regularly stayed at The Woodward Hotel now The Best Western Woodward. Two blocks down was The Birdland Club, probably the most famous jazz club in the world.

'I remember going there to see Canonball Adderly whose records I had collected at home. I was sitting on my own at a table and when he had finished his piece on alto sax he came down and sat beside me. When he heard my accent, he commented:

'You're not from the States, man, are you?'

'No, I'm from Ireland,' replied an overawed Cole.

'Are you off one of the boats in here, or somethin''?'

'Ah . . . yes, that's right, I'm off one of the boats,' Cole gulped.

'I was in such awe of this guy that I wouldn't even admit I was a musician and a sax player even though I had played to 2,500 people round in the City Center Ballroom while he had only a few dozen listeners. He asked me about the jazz scene in Ireland, and then he was off back on stage to do his next piece. He has since died.'

Another night the entire Capitol Showband went to The Birdland for a few drinks after they had finished playing in The City Center Ballroom.

'I remember this midget of a manager with a big cigar used to pass by with a red rose in his lapel. It was disconcerting because he would pass you at a very low level in the dark with this enormous cigar alight. The great Dizzy Gillespie was playing there and during the interval he joined us for a few drinks. Our fellows, living up to their reputation, poured drink into him and he got nicely merry and refused to go back on stage.

"Fuck off, man, I'm with my Irish friends!" he used to yell at the little fellow when he tried to get him to go back to do his show. He kept shouting "Erin go brágh" because he used to see those words written up on banners in New York on St Patrick's Day. I wasn't drinking at the time, so I went over and pleaded with him to go back and to ignore the boys. Eventually he went back on stage, very drunk, but was still able to play.'

Cole also went round to The Metropole bar where the band played behind the bar.

'Gene Krupa, the famous drummer had a big band in there — a row of saxophones, a row of trumpets, a row of trombones and so on. If you wanted to listen to the trombones, you sat in front of that row. If you wanted to hear the whole band, the best place to sit was out on the sidewalk. I used to sit in front of the sax players. Gene Krupa might only be playing to an audience of 100, while we would have had anything up to 3,000 round at the City Center Ballroom.'

When Paddy Cole went into semi-retirement, following the break-up of the Superstars, he and Helen made an annual trip to the Cork Guinness Jazz Festival. He never forgot to bring his sax and clarinet with him for blows with guest musicians.

'Pat Horgan, a member of the organising committee, was a great help to me in breaking into the Cork jazz scene. He put me into the Metropole as a star guest. That was a tough gig because I had to sit in with fully rehearsed bands. They resented this as well.'

Horgan urged Cole to go round and sit in with the bands he knew as a guest attraction. The Jazz Coasters from Dublin were playing in Jury's Hotel and Paddy went round to join them. They refused to allow him to play. It was a major embarrassment for Cole. His old colleague, Paul Sweeney, who played trumpet with the Coasters, was disgusted.

'I had more difficulties with the Jazz Coasters. Some time later when the Gay Byrne Radio Show was coming from Grafton Street, Joe Duffy, who was then a researcher, asked me to come along and sit in with the Coasters for one of the Christmas shows. I got up and drove from Castleblaney to Dublin for 8.45 a.m. I arrived in Bewley's but noticed I was getting a complete put-off from the Coasters, including the band leader, Kevin Hayes.'

Cole approached him.

'Kevin,' he asked, 'what number are we doing?'

'You are not doing any number with us,' snapped Hayes. 'You never phoned me to clear it that you could play with the band.'

Cole tried to explain that he presumed the programme organisers had done all the preparatory work, including telling the Jazz Coasters that Paddy Cole was playing, but it was no use.

The negotiations continued in Bewley's. With just minutes to go to transmission, Jack Daly, the drummer, threatened to walk out of the programme if Cole played. Paul Sweeney packed his trumpet and said he was leaving in sympathy with Cole. The scene was chaotic.

Suddenly Gay Byrne appeared and shouted: 'Paddy, you and the boys are next.' Cole mounted the bandstand, set up outside Donal McNally, Opticians. Daly still insisted he would not play.

'They strung me out to the very last. It was one of the worst experiences I ever had. I had apologised profusely. I would never treat anybody like that. To rub salt into their wounds, Gay introduced us as "The Jazz Coasters with Paul Sweeney and Paddy Cole".

'Afterwards the boys in the band were all sweetness to me again and invited me around for a drink in Neary's, but I declined the offer. I left with Helen and Paul Sweeney and his wife, Catherine, and we went elsewhere. It was just another example of Dublin musicians trying to keep the scene tight among themselves.'

Ironically, some years later Kevin Hayes phoned Cole to ask him to help organise a fund-raising venture in Athlone. He wanted Paddy Cole on the basis that while the Jazz Coasters would play, the Paddy Cole Band would draw the crowd. The gig never happened.

The attitude of the Coasters was typical of many of the resident bands in Dublin to outsiders coming in. According to Cole, the resentment is still there.

'They don't like fellows like myself coming to Dublin and managing to make a living out of the business. They thought the scene was their own. Now they complain that there are so few jazz venues. But they killed it themselves. That's why many of them are not working now. Remember Count Basey recorded *The Hucklebuck*.'

'There used to be an old fallacy about jazz musicians sitting drinking pints all night, and looking very dishevelled. I was once sitting in a London hotel having an early breakfast when Dave Brubeck's band walked in, all dressed immaculately. I could not believe it as these were the top jazz players in the world. It blew the whole fallacy out of the water. I came back to Dublin to see fellows hanging out of double-basses with long, scraggy hair.

'But it must be frustrating to people who pioneered the jazz scene in Dublin. We are a working band. We play jazz. We play '60s rock and roll. We also play an old time waltz if the people want it. That's why we're working today. You have to be versatile.'

Gay Byrne, a jazz enthusiast all his life, agrees that it is impossible for a jazz band to survive in Ireland. He originally got into RTE radio through a programme called *Jazz Corner*, which was broadcast on Monday nights.

'At that time jazz was frowned upon by Radio Eireann, and was frequently referred to as "nigger music",' he recalls. 'It was alien to our culture.

'Adrian Cronin, who was also a jazz fan, and myself set up the Blue Note Jazz Club on St Stephen's Green, but it has always been a minority interest, and there is nobody going to make a living out of it in this country. The market for modern jazz is very small. What market there is there is for traditional jazz. It's just happy music that people want and that's what Paddy and the band play. People respond to a happy sound. But there are people in jazz who look down on Paddy Cole and trad men because they say that's "umpty umpty" music. There is always this jealousy and argument among musicians.'

Back at the Cork Guinness Jazz Festival, Paddy Cole had put together his own band and was booked to play in Jury's Hotel, but there was more trouble ahead. In the year he was booked to play, Galway manager Dick Burke replaced the former manager, Peter Malone, who moved to Jury's in Dublin. Burke decided to bring a jazz band from Galway.

'I got a phone call to say I was not playing in Jury's. I went bananas because this was the last minute and all our plans were made. Pat Horgan was annoyed as well, but suggested that Gerry O'Connor, who had started the Sunday lunchtime jazz session in Acton's Hotel in Kinsale, might be interested in having jazz in his new hotel, the Blarney Park.'

O'Connor was not sure it would work because Blarney is a good distance outside the city.

'At that time Blarney was not included in the jazz trail at all,' says Gerry O'Connor. 'I was looking around but there were no major acts available. Out the blue I got a call saying Paddy Cole might be interested. I hadn't met Paddy before, but I knew he was a guy you could talk straight to. We worked out a deal on the telephone in five minutes. I have dealt with a lot of musicians over the years, but I don't know anybody as straightforward to deal with as Paddy.'

One of the effects of Cole's arrival in the Blarney Park Hotel was to move the Jazz Festival to venues outside the city. That was in 1987 and the rest is history. Paddy Cole is a fixture for the Jazz Festival in the Blarney Park, where he draws a loyal, regular following. Even the bar is named after him, with a pictorial biography on the wall. The idea was to pay tribute to a living legend, rather than one who has passed away. Centrepiece of the display on Cole's long and varied career is the Silver Disc, presented to him in Galway in 1984 by K-Tel for the sales of his album, *Music Man.*

Jazzing it up at the Cork Guinness Jazz Festival with Gerry O'Connor, proprietor of the Blarney Park Hotel and his wife, Elizabeth.

'Like Brian McGill in the Harcourt Hotel,' says Cole, 'Gerry O'Connor gave the jazz weekend his full commitment. He was fighting an uphill battle but he publicised the jazz at the Blarney Park. The first year was quiet, except for the Saturday night, but the next year the place was booked out. It's now one of the highlights of our year. We play the Friday night, Saturday night, Sunday lunchtime, Sunday night and Monday lunchtime. All the sessions are packed. Guinness also extended the jazz trail to the outlying areas. Without realising it, Dick Burke did me the best turn of my life.

The Guinness Jazz Festival also provides an opportunity to meet old friends. Often it's the only opportunity. Walking down Patrick St during the Festival in 1994, Paddy Cole encountered his long-time hero, Johnny Quigley from Derry. There, too, were the Jazz Lads from Sligo, bringing back memories of Strandhill and its late night sessions. There was even the chance to meet old friends from Dublin, like the Closkey/Hopkins jazz band, who make the annual trip to the south for the October Bank Holiday weekend.

Marco Petrassi, the trumpet player with the Cork City Jazz Band, is a special friend of Cole's since the days he played with Maurice Mulcahy. During his long career in the business Petrassi has played with 32 different bands.

A special feature of the Jazz weekend is the farewell get-together in Acton's Hotel on Monday afternoon when Paddy Cole, Sonny Knowles and Cork's own Joe Mac join Marco, Billy Crosbie and all the the Cork City Jazz Band for a final session. 'It's a sort of jamboree finale to the Festival,' says Cole.

The Guinness Jazz Festival is known all over the world.

'When I go to New Orleans each Autumn, musicians come up to us and say they know about the jazz in Cork and how much they would like to go there. An invite to the Guinness Jazz Festival is a prized possession for many musicians in the States.'

The festival is now Cork's biggest tourism weekend. Will it stay in the southern capital? Paddy Cole's answer is a definite 'Yes'.

'It's completely associated with Cork now and is very well run. The venue is ideal, with the Opera House for the visiting guests and the Jazz Trail for the fans. I don't think it could be moved now. If some of the jazz musicians I know in Dublin got their hands on it, it would not survive. I think it's safer in Cork.

'As well as that, I have always been good friends with the Guinness people and, in particular with Brian Brown, who runs the Jazz Festival and the Managing Director, Colin Storm.'

Apart from the Guiness Jazz Festival, Paddy Cole is a regular guest at the Howth Jazz Festival at Easter, the Adare Jazz Festival on St Patrick's weekend and the Dungarvan Jazz Festival on Valentine's weekend.

In Adare, the Paddy Cole Band decided to throw in a '60s medley for variety and the crowd loved it. One enthusiastic fan came up to Paddy and said: 'Good man yourself, Paddy, that's the kind of jazz we like to hear'!

'Jazz is the sort of music that fits in anywhere. It's ideal for weddings, garden parties, and receptions,' says Cole. 'The music goes down particularly well at the Budweiser Derby and Punchestown Races.'

He has even made it a must at the launch of Mitsubishi and BMW cars!

'We were invited to play in Seaman's Garage in Cork for the launch of Mitsubishi's new Pajero jeep in 1992. It was supposed to be just a simple cheese and wine reception, but as soon as we started playing the thing developed into a dance. We played for two or three hours. Frank Keane, Paddy Murphy and Eugene O'Reilly of BMW/Mitsubishi still talk about it. It's all because jazz is a happy type of music and it makes people feel good.' Cole's distinctive musical style also makes the band a big hit each year in Mosney where Paddy and the boys have been guests of Felim McCloskey for the past eight years.

The capital of Dixieland jazz is, of course, New Orleans, and although he had often been to many parts of the United States, Paddy Cole didn't get there until 1990. It came about by accident.

Cole had played golf in Royal Dublin with Sean Griffin of Sean Griffin Travel who asked him if he had ever been to New Orleans. A deal was quickly worked out whereby Paddy Cole accompanied an annual trip each year to the mecca of the jazz world. The deal was that Paddy and the band would bring their instruments and play a few sessions. These days, New Orleans is aimed at the tourist market, but there are still living legends playing there.

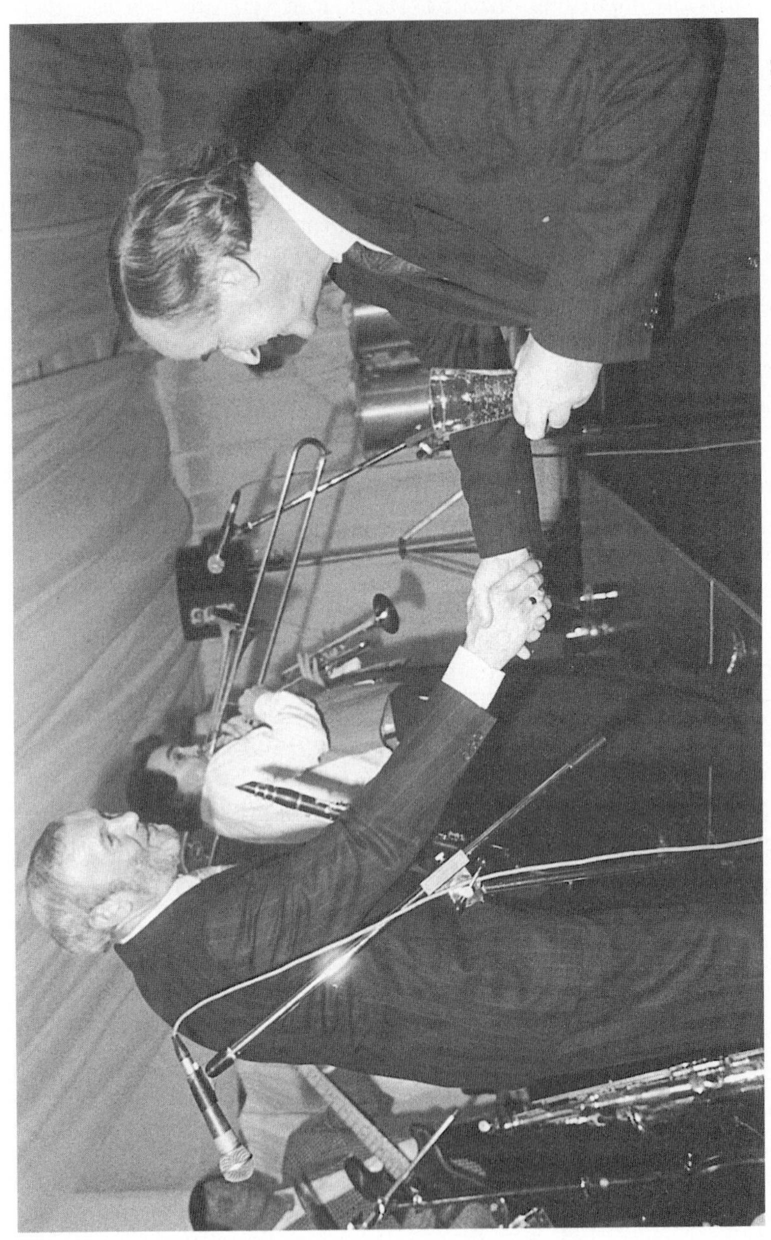

Meeting an old friend from the showband days. Paddy is greeted by former Taoiseach Albert Reynolds at the opening of Eamonn Monahan's showrooms in Dublin.

'There people come to listen to jazz with their eyes. If they see an old black guy playing, then they reckon he has got to be the real thing. There, too, is Sachmo Park, dedicated to Louis Armstrong, and great clubs like Maxwells. Any night you go to Maxwells, you are guaranteed to hear good jazz. Harry Connick Snr plays there a few nights a week and Rene Nato, one of the finest clarinet players I have ever heard, has his own band there.'

The trips have not been without their lighter moments.

In 1994 Cole travelled out a few days early to enjoy some golf at the magnificent Sea Island Plantation in Georgia. Tired and exhausted, he arrived at the top rated Cloister Hotel late at night, a regular holiday resort of the Kennedy family. The hotel was full and Cole ended up sharing a room with Paul McMenamin, who is with the Smurfit Corporation.

'The guy had gone out for a few beers when I checked in so I went straight to bed. I was into a deep, heavy sleep when I was woken up by this fellow saying: "Hi, boy, what the fuck are you doing here? You're in the wrong room. Scram!" And he had the door open.

'I explained to him who I was and that we were sharing. So he shook hands and said he was delighted to see me. "Now, don't you wake up and have a good sleep,' he declared. I was dropping off to sleep again when this snoring started. This guy snored like nothing on earth. He rattled the walls. I got up, looked about and found a huge walk-in wardrobe in the room. I took the cushions from the sofa, spread them in the wardrobe, went inside and lay down. And there I was, trying to sleep on the floor of a wardrobe in this magnificent, old world hotel. Even inside the wardrobe I could still hear him.

'The next morning Paul was very embarrassed and apologised. That night we were out for a few beers and while I was having a shower before bed, Paul disappeared — into the wardrobe. We took turns in sleeping in the wardrobe!'

The co-ordinator of the golf outing was Dublin PR man Kevin Norton who, along with Paddy, spotted a sale of silk ties in the Sea

Island Golf Club house. The ties were variously priced from $10 up to $70.

'How much for the lot?' enquired Norton, half jokingly.

'Oh, I suppose $150,' mused the salesman.

'Done!' shouted Norton.

And with that, Norton and Cole emptied the two wicker baskets of ties into a large refuse sack against the protests of the hapless salesman who thought Norton was only joking. There were presents of silk ties all round for everybody on the trip.

Cole's pilgrimage to New Orleans may have been delayed, but playing jazz took Cole to Doha and Dubai in 1981. The trip was arranged by his sister, Lucia, who presented radio and TV shows in Doha.

'I used to play a lot of Paddy's music on both radio and TV and listeners started to ring in, asking "Where can we buy records of this fellow Cole?". One day I said after a record: "That was Big Brother Paddy" and the phones really started hopping. Eventually a group who ran the Doha Club came to me and asked would Paddy and the band come out. I had a terrible job tracking him down, but eventually they all came out in 1991.'

The band stayed in the Renaissance Hotel managed by Gordon McKenzie, a Scottish man. It was mainly an ex-pats clientele, but there were some Muslims. too. There was one worry on the minds of Paddy Cole and the band before they set out.

'About this trip,' said Paddy on the phone to Lucia one night, 'how are we fixed for booze in a Muslim country? The boys are very worried about this.' Lucia assured him that there was more booze there than they would need.

The night they arrived in Doha, the band were guests of the Turkish ambassador at a spectacular open-air fashion show. Fears that they would not see a woman for the duration of the trip were quickly scotched when some scantily clad Turkish belly-dancers took the stage.

'Jimmy Hogan was not a well man after looking at them!' Lucia recalls.

During the trip the American Ambassador to Qatar presented Paddy with an award because of his American links over the years.

'It was a very impressive function,' says Lucia. 'The Ambassador was presenting awards to scientists, veterans of the Gulf War and many other distinguished people, and there among them all was Paddy and this Irish band, all dressed up for the occasion. I was so proud of them.'

During a trip across the desert the band came across a caravan of Bedouin Arabs on the move, complete with camels and spectacular dress. It was one of the highlights of Paddy Cole's career, meeting the tribe in the middle of the desert. They had seen pictures in the papers, seen it on TV, and here was the real thing.

Paddy and Jimmy Hogan make friends with some camels during the filming of a TV special in the desert.

'One of the things we noticed about them was that the little guys had webbed feet and webbed hands,' says Lucia. 'Their feet had adapted to walking on the sand.' The band went to play a special gig for handicapped children in the Rumailaih hospital, with the local people turning out to dance to their music.

Jazz enables Paddy Cole to combine holidays and work. Like the New Orleans trips, the Joe Cuddy golf classics run by Seán Skehan are another highlight of the calendar. The trips to Spain have seen some fine impromptu performances, including the finest finale to a Cabaret sport Cole has ever witnessed.

'One night, at the end of his spot Joe Cuddy sang *New York, New York* and people gathered on the balconies overhead to listen to him. While waiting for the music to finish, Joe jumped into the swimming pool fully clothed and still wearing a carnation, swam up and down the full length of the pool before getting out again on cue to sing the last *New York, New York*. It was the best finale I have ever seen. Then I heard one of the lads saying: "Cole's next". I grabbed my sax and fled.'

But the swimming pool did not provide such a happy finale for Eric Nolan. Renowned for organising huge charity functions in London, Nolan used to dress up as an Arab just for the fun of it.

'He and his pals, Gerry Smithers and Brendan McBride, used to hire limousines and arrive at the best restaurant in town where Nolan would be ushered in as a distinguished Arab sheik. He would wear worry beads and "pray" as he went along. People would stand to one side and let him pass. Then, suddenly, he would jump up on a table throw off the Arab attire and sing *Danny Boy* to the consternation of all present!'

For devilment, on one of the Joe Cuddy classics in Spain, people were thrown into the pool. Nolan, very much against his wishes, was thrown in, but could not swim.

'Eric shouted at me that he couldn't swim, but I froze with fright. However, another guy, John O'Reilly, who was Des Smyth's caddy, jumped in and grabbed him. He lay there on the side of the pool spluttering, but survived. It was a close shave.'

Eric Nolan died subsequently in early 1995.

Back in Castleblaney in 1987 Cole was instrumental in securing a Northern Ireland tourism award for a Northern Ireland garage owner.

'On November 25 I had driven to Comber, Co Down to a specialist to investigate the ongoing back problem. When I came out on the street afterwards my car would not start. I was already pressed for time as I had a gig in Dundalk later that night. As always, the gig came first. I went down the road to a garage. Comber Commercials, where a guy, Raymond Stanex, immediately offered me his car although he did not know who I was. Off I went.

The Paddy Cole winning team on the Joe Cuddy Golf Classic in Spain in September 1988 — Peter Gaw, Rhona Teehan, Joe Cuddy and Brendan O'Flaherty. The trip is an annual event run by Sean Skehan, another old friend of Paddy's.

'Later I was telling the lads in the band about it and the word reached RTE. The next morning the incident was featured by Gaybo on his radio programme as an example of the goodwill in Northern Ireland which contrasted with all the bad news that came out of the province. When I brought the car back to Stanex, he had already heard me being interviewed by Gaybo. He subsequently received an award from the Northern Ireland Tourism Board.'

12
AT LAST I'M A MOVIE STAR

A New York cinema, 1991. Hundreds of Irish/Americans are watching a new hit film entitled *Hear My Song*, based loosely on the singer Joseph Locke. Suddenly Paddy Cole, who has a small part in the movie, appears on screen playing the clarinet in a close-up shot.

Down in the middle of the audience, Frank McElroy, originally from Castleblaney, recognises his old school pal. He jumps up with excitement and shouts: 'Hey, I know that guy. He's a pal of mine'.

Immediately a hand from the row behind roughly pulls him roughly backwards.

'Sit down, you bum!' says an angry voice.

(McElroy had regularly met Paddy Cole during his trips to the US, and once organised a "job" for him whereby Cole would go a certain building site each morning and sign on, but never actually do any work.)

The movie *Hear My Song* attained almost cult status in Irish–American community when it was released in 1991.

Paddy Cole's film career began with a phone call from former Cadets showband star Eileen Reid. She rang in the run-up to the making of *The Commitments*, to tell him the producer was looking for a sax player. A number of people had suggested Cole would be ideal for the part of Joey The Lip.

'Eileen asked me to go to Ross Hubbard's office on Landsdowne Road on the following Monday, but as I was living in Castleblaney, I did not get there until Wednesday. When I arrived they gave me a piece to read and filmed it. I hardly knew what I was doing, but they were very pleased with it. Suddenly Ross's brother walked in and said: "I'm sorry, Paddy, but the director, Alan Parker, has been on to say they are going to use an actor as a trumpet player".'

Paddy Cole's movie career appeared to have ended before it started. However, a few days later, agent Margaret Nolan, telephoned from Dublin to say there were auditions going on for another film, *Hear My Song* in which there was a 20 second slot for a three-piece band, including a clarinet. She suggested that Cole audition for it.

Two days later saw Paddy Cole in a queue outside Windmill Lane studios with other hopefuls, including Frank Kelly and Joe Cuddy. After his audition, a delighted Cuddy came and told Cole he was in. Finally, Paddy's turn came.

'Inside in this little theatre the director, Peter Chelsom, was sitting with his assistant. He looked completely pissed off, after a long, boring day.

"So what part are you in for, then,?" asked a seemingly disinterested Chelsom.

"I don't know," replied Cole tersely.

"What?" said Chelsom.

'I was pissed off as well, after all the waiting, so I said to him: "Look, if it gives you a clue, I play the clarinet. If that suits you, OK. If it doesn't, that's OK as well".'

Chelsom burst out laughing, turned to his assistant, and said: 'I think this guy could fill a bigger role. He could be one of Joe Locke's pals'. The assistant nodded in agreement. Cole got the part, and was given a bound copy of the script.

'When I came out Joe Cuddy and myself went around to the Docker's pub and threw the bound copies on the counter to let everybody know we had landed the parts.

'What part did you get, Paddy?' asked Cuddy.

'I haven't a clue, Joe', replied Cole. 'All I know is that I'm a pal of Joseph Locke's. 'What did you get?'

Cuddy said he was supposed to play the part of a pretty dreadful singer named Frank Cinatra, who did the round of working men's clubs in the North of England.

'I'm supposed to sing out of tune and be off key most of the time,' said Cuddy.

'Well, Joe, you're made for that part!' replied Cole, before bursting into laughter.

A few weeks later, Paddy Cole arrived at 7a.m., as arranged, outside a pub in the Strawberry Beds outside Dublin for his first scene in the movie (the tooth-pulling scene).

'The place was a hive of activity. There were trucks and lights everywhere. Nobody paid a bit of heed in me, so eventually after half an hour I told a young assistant who I was.

"Go to make-up straight away. You should have been here half an hour ago,' she snapped.

They dressed me up in farmer's gear of the '30s, an old cap, wellingtons, the lot. My ego swelled, I thought to myself: "Here comes another Paul Newman".'

Cole went into the pub and on to the set. Waiting was the director, Peter Chelsom, and leading actors Ned Beatty, who played the part of Joe Locke, and Adrian Dunbarr who played the part of Micky O'Neill. Dunbarr had co-written the script. The shooting commenced.

'I never had such fun in all my life. It was unbelievable and one of the peaks I look back on with great affection. Joe Cuddy was excellent. '

Filming meant Paddy Cole had to reschedule his gigs, or try and fit them in with filming.

'I remember being chauffeur-driven up to the Abbeyglen Hotel in Clifden, Co. Galway one Monday morning after finishing in the Harcourt, and arriving at 6.30a.m.

Paul Hughes, the owner was there to greet me. I went up to my room and could not wait to get into bed I was so tired. I was just in it when Paul rang to say my car was leaving in ten minutes. I was out of bed again and into a boat. We spent the whole day in the boat and only for the freezing cold, I would have fallen asleep.'

In the film, Paddy Cole had three words to say: "She never left". The words were in response to a question from Ned Beatty about a boat, aboard which he had earlier escaped from England.

'I never knew there were so many ways of saying "She never left". You can emphasise the "she", the "never", or the "left". Ronan Collins was on RTE radio doing the variations, adding: "These are the words of the famous thespian from Co. Monaghan, Paddy Cole". The boys in the band were sick listening to me.'

Every Sunday night, while the filming was underway the entire cast and crew regularly arrived at the Harcourt Hotel for the Sunday night jazz session. Reggie Lloyd, the bass player, had a part in the film also.

'John Altman, the musical director was a fabulous sax player and used to sit in with us. So too did actor Adrian Dunbarr on bass. Dunbarr was a native of Enniskillen and had played bass with Cecil Kettle and the Sky Rockets among other bands.'

On the night of the Dublin premiere, Paddy Cole arrived at the Savoy cinema accompanied by Helen, his mother and all his sisters. When the three famous words 'She never left' were spoken on screen, a huge cheer rang out from the audience.

'Peter Chelsom was like a god to us during the making of that film. He had so many things on his mind that if he spoke to you on the set you felt very important. I thought he was one of the most controlled, organised people with whom I have ever worked. He showed immense patience with guys like me, who had never been on a film set before and probably spent most of the time getting in the way and talking and laughing when we should be silent. I have the height of admiration for him since, and for Adrian.

'I still hear from Peter Chelsom. The last card I got from him was a picture of his wife and newly born baby with the caption: "This kid still doesn't even understand basic algebra".'

Old friends together at a special RTE fund-raiser for GOAL in January 1990. From left: Joe Dolan, Derek Dean, Paddy Cole, Fr Brian D'Arcy, Brendan O'Brien, Joe Mac, Earl Gill, Sean Dunphy, Sonny Knowles, Jimmy McGee. In front: Bibi Baskin and John O'Shea. At the piano is Eamonn Monahan.

These days Paddy Cole is delighted to see so many new films being made in Ireland.

'The film industry has really taken off in Ireland, particularly with the tax breaks, and it has opened up a whole new world. In my view this country is an ideal location for film-making and there is top class talent available. There is no reason why Dublin and Ireland cannot become a mini-Hollywood in the years ahead.'

13

YES, SIR, THAT'S MY TV SERIES

Wednesday 7 June, 1995. It's eight o'clock in the evening in Galway's Great Southern Hotel, and Paddy Cole, dressed in a smart Louis Copeland jacket and trousers, is warming up the audience for his first ever TV series. He puts the audience in the mood with the well known jazz number, *Yes Sir, That's My Baby,* and the recording gets under way. Cole and his band swing into another popular jazz standard, *You Scream, I Scream*. The tune is in the same key, and has the same chord sequence as *Yes Sir, That's My Baby.* After the clarinet solo Cole mistakenly goes back into the warm-up number, *Yes, Sir.....* The recording comes to a sudden halt. Cole turns to the audience and laughs: 'What a feckin' start to a TV series!'

Getting your own television series is the career ambition of any musician or entertainer. It is an acknowledgement that 'you've made it' and are now a nationally recognised figure in the showbiz world, capable of attracting a large audience. In Paddy Cole's case the series came relatively late in his career. He had, after all, hung up his saxophone and clarinet in the early '80s and retired from the business. His successful comeback in a highly competitive business where thousands have failed, is a tribute to his dedication and talent.

Craic 'n' Cole came about through John McColgan, a former senior television producer with RTE and the MD of the independent Tyrone Productions.

'When John was a senior producer in RTE, he had always said I should have my own show,' says Cole. 'He had given me a guest spot on many shows he produced, and when he moved to the BBC I was very sorry to see him go.

'For example, John had been instrumental in getting Colm Wilkinson the part in *Jesus Christ Superstar* in London. He had great foresight and imagination. Colm rehearsed for the audition in John's apartment and John accompanied him to the rehearsals. His wife, Moya Doherty, was the woman behind *Riverdance*, probably the greatest musical production to come out of this country. It must be unique that two such talented people are in the same household.'

The original idea behind *Craic 'n' Cole* was to go around the country and film a series of ten programmes in pubs, using local talent. McColgan approached RTE and they liked the idea.

'One morning McColgan phoned me and said RTE had given the go-ahead for a series of recordings around the country. At first I didn't believe it and started laughing. When I realised this was for real, I started to panic. Would I be able for this? How would I present it?

'McColgan advised me: "Just be yourself". So I said, there's no point in me trying to be Gay Byrne because I'm not a professional presenter. I had a long chat with my old pal, Ronan Collins and he, too, gave me some good advice.'

The ten-part series proved a winner, with an enthusiastic response from viewers and high TAM ratings, despite having to compete with the 1995 summer heatwave.

'The biggest critics of the show were ourselves, particularly me,' says Cole. 'When at home, I used to watch it in a room on my own. I couldn't watch it with other people.'

In the series, Paddy was joined by his regular band, together with Chris Conevey on keyboards, Carl Geraghty on saxophone, plus Mick Nolan and Steve McDonald on trumpet. The musical director was Jack Bayle, the regular trombone-player in Cole's band. 'Jack did a great job on the show,' says Cole. 'There were nights when he went home from gigs, stayed up all night working on arrangements for the visiting acts, and then went straight into rehearsals.'

Paddy Cole is primarily associated with Dixieland jazz music, but his taste extends to country and traditional music.

Paddy Cole and his current band. From left: Neil McKenna, Johnny Christopher, Jack Bayle, Reggie Lloyd and Jimmy Hogan.

'County music is knocked a lot, but the old story holds true — the guys who were doing it well have survived, like Ray Lynam, Big Tom, Hugo Duncan, Susan McCann and Philomena Begley.

There were a lot of people who jumped on the bandwagon, as during the showband days. I wrongly got the name of being anti-country music whereas, in fact, I have a huge collection of the records of Waylon Jennings and Willie Nelson. I was introduced to their music by my brother-in-law, Ronnie Duffy, the drummer with the Mainliners, and through listening to Neil Toner's radio show.'

When the Paddy Cole Superstars recorded an album, it was RTE country music DJ, Paschal Mooney, who suggested that they feature bass player Mike Dalton singing *Good Hearted Woman*. 'The one thing that does irritate me is Country 'n' Irish music. There is obviously a market for that sort of music but I am not into it at all.'

Cole also remembers another very popular band, The Smoky Mountain Ramblers. 'On stage they looked the most disinterested band I have ever seen, and they probably were because they were just on a wage. There was no variety and eventually the band just ground to a halt. Like jazz bands, I don't think a country band can get away with just doing country music any more.

'Daniel O'Donnell has, of course, lifted country music on to a new plain, and carried a lot of guys with him. He is a credit to the industry, and one of the most professional guys I have seen at work. He leaves nothing to chance. He is also the best PR man in the business and regularly spends an hour or more talking to fans after his shows and signing autographs. He knows many of his fans by name.'

RTE's Ronan Collins is more critical of the way country music has developed.

'Daniel O'Donnell does well, but he doesn't do well for anybody else. He comes in and cleans out an area. He takes the admission fee, the money for the T-shirts, the videos and the tapes and the people are left with nothing else. That's what Garth Brooks has done in America with country music. He has just cleaned out the audience and there's nothing left for anybody else.

'Just because someone is successful does not mean they are good, or that they are the best at what they do. Paddy Cole has not gone on to the larger stage. He has a band who are not young fellows, but they are all working musicians and he looks after them well. He is a classic example of the notion that if something is worth doing, it is worth doing yourself.'

Cole has a particular fondness for Irish music and is delighted by its resurgence in recent years. In his time with the Capitol Showband, he came to know and appreciate the music played in the halls in Fulham by two Irishmen, John Bowe on accordion and Roger Sherlock on flute. These men played Irish music when it was not popular with the public.

'*Riverdance*, composed by Bill Whelan, is the biggest thing that has happened Irish music in my lifetime,' says Cole. 'It is a huge opportunity to show Irish music to the world. As a young boy growing up in Castleblaney, I danced in the local feiseanna. In those days you were told to keep your hands down by your sides, to hold your head erect, and not to look left or right. You were like a pole on the stage. But *Riverdance* has put great flair into dancing. What impressed me more than anything were the musicians in the band. I was very proud of them.'

Long before *Riverdance*, of course, the Chieftains were flying the flag and Cole pays them tribute. 'They are great ambassadors for Ireland and for Irish music and culture. I am a particular fan of Paddy Maloney and Matt Molloy. The Dubliners, too, are legends all over the world. Everywhere I go, I hear people talking about them. Ronnie Drew, a very old friend of mine, has more stories told about him than anyone in the business. Like the time he was sitting in a pub in Blackrock in Dublin, when he wasn't supposed to be drinking. It was about 11.30 in the morning and he was there with a dozen others, all having a "cure" from the night before. This loud-mouth walking by, spotted Ronnie and gave him an unmerciful slap on the back, which nearly floored him.

"Good man, Ronnie!" he shouted, "I thought you weren't supposed to be drinking". Of course, everybody immediately looked down the counter.

But Ronnie had his answer ready: "I have a bottle of stout and a half one every morning, and it helps me to mind my own business. You should try it!"

'Another time, Eamonn Monahan and myself met him at Leopardstown Races. He was on crutches with a broken leg, but had still managed to get jarred. He was propped up against a wall, unable to go one way or the other.

"Ronnie, are you all right?" we asked. "Well, lads", he said. "If I'd known I was going to live this long, I'd have looked after myself an awful lot better!"

Other performers who won the Cole seal of approval include Altan, Stockton's Wing, Four Men and a Dog and Dolores Keane. 'Sharon Shanon has given a new credibility to box playing as has Mairtin O'Connor from Galway, who is in *Riverdance*. I particularly like the blend of traditional and modern music, like when Richie Buckley, one of our top jazz sax players, sits in with Sharon Shanon. There is a great blend of music at the moment.

'On my nights off I might go along to the Harcourt Hotel to see and listen to Sean Maguire, the fiddle player, Paddy Glacken, Sean Potts and Ray Lynam. Years ago, when the outside bands were resented by the resident Dublin bands, one member of the Potts family, Eddie, was a gentle giant who used to talk to us about instruments in an otherwise often hostile bandroom. Eddie was one of life's gentlemen.

'Arty McGlynn played with all the showbands around Omagh and is now one of the most respected traditional players on string instruments, and always in demand.

Journalist/broadcaster Nell McCafferty also features high on Paddy Cole's list of favourite people.

A few years ago I was walking down Leeson Street on my way to a firm of accountants when I met Nell looking for the Well Woman Centre.

"Come in here with me to the accountancy office. They'll know where it is," I said helpfully. In we went.

The girls behind the counter told us it was three doors down the street.

"There you go, Nell," I declared, "It's three doors down."

"Oh, typical you," shouted Nell, "You land me in trouble and then you won't even come in with me. Shame on you." And she stormed out of the office.

'The girls in the office gave me some very strange looks,' says Cole.

Apart from music, how does Paddy Cole relax? Golfing and fishing, in that order. 'My father taught me how to fish and it's a great thing for any youngster to learn. I recently read where a Dublin teacher takes his class to the canal once a week to teach them how to fish. I said to myself: "Now that's a guy with foresight because a big percentage of that class will never get jobs. That teacher is wisely planning for how they will spend their leisure time".

'A first cousin of mine, Tommy Walsh, who later played trumpet with the Millionaires showband, and Denis Hughes used to spend many hours fishing. My father taught us the tricks of the sport, the best times to fish and how to encourage them to bite. I still fish, but I don't have as much time to give to it as I would like.'

Paddy Cole, on his own admission, is no Christy O'Connor.

'I first learned to play golf with the Capitol Showband. Sean 'The Spoofer' Jordan made us go out on the course and practise, just for exercise. When in Cork, he used to bring us out to Little Island and Douglas. Butch Moore loved the sun and would strip down to his shorts. But the Spoofer used to go bananas. Golf, he stressed, was a game of honour, and the etiquette on the golf course made it pleasant for everybody else. So Butch would have to put his shirt on again.

'But Butch, Johnny Kelly and myself used to think guys who played golf were mad. I spent five years in Las Vegas, but I never played there, even though we had the finest courses at our disposal. I now regard those years as lost. Golf is a great social game, and I look forward to it more than anything else.'

Cole has played for many years with the Links Golfing Society, a charity body, organised by Cecil Whelan. The Society has raised many thousands of pounds for charity over the years. 'A lot of the guys in the business play golf — Joe Dolan, Red Hurley, Dickie Rock, Paul Sweeney, Dermot O'Brien, Cathy Durkan, comedians like Al Banim, Syl Fox, Frank Carson and Gene Fitzpatrick, as well as Niall Toibín, The Furey Brothers, Jim Doherty and Donie Cassidy.

When I am away in the country, I ring up old friends for a game, guys such as Roddy Gillen, from the Jazz Lads in Sligo, or Billy Crosbie, from the Cork City Jazz Band, both great at the game.

'I admit that my clarinet, rather than me, gets invited to many functions. People say to me: "Paddy, would you play golf on such a date, and bring along your clarinet". I say I'll bring the clarinet along to show I can play something!"

'But it's a great opportunity to get away from it all, and to relax with some of my friends outside of the business, like Martin McArdle and Tony Gilroy from Superquinn. I also go to Donabate and play with Paddy McNally, Jim Clinton, Micky Gilmartin, Tom Breslin, Evan Henry and Kevin Beahan, the famous Louth footballer. The Spoofer Jordan is a member there, and we still play together. My golf is improving, but I'm still standing too close to the ball after I hit it!'

A regular playing partner is Ronan Collins, together with his brothers, Michael and Mark. All three are good at the game and play off very low handicaps.

'Paddy's golf is very erratic.' says Collins, 'Sometimes you wonder how he can hit the ball at all, standing the way he does! He plays golf like he does everything else, with gusto and enthusiasm, and he's great company on the golf course. In fact, he's great company anywhere.'

'The strange thing about Ronan Collins,' says Cole, 'is that while he does everything right, I can still manage to win the money off him!'

'Paddy should stick to music,' says Joe Dolan, another regular partner. 'He certainly wouldn't make a living from playing golf.'

Cole, a regular at Croke Park, is a keen all-round sports fan. Right now he's delighted at the emergence of Irish sports women on the international scene, and predicts that Sonia O'Sullivan and Michelle Smith, will both win gold in the Atlanta Olympics. He has also been involved in fund-raising for the 1996 Paralympics.

What of the future? He has no intention of retiring yet. Now 55, he is happy to continue doing what he knows best, playing music and being an entertainer. He is a simple man who likes the simple things in life. As a musician, he is a superb clarinetist and a great sax player. But above all, he is an entertainer.

When it comes to singing, it is as well he has a clarinet to play, jokes Ronan Collins. 'If you had a power drill that sounded like that, you'd get it fixed!'

Joe Dolan is equally unflattering.

'Paddy Cole the SINGER? You're joking!', he says. 'But he's one hell of a musician and also one of the nicest guys in the business.'

Dolan recalls a big favour Cole did for him in 1968, when he had brought out his hit single, *Make Me an Island.*

'My band had broken up and I needed to do a little promotion in London. The Capitol Showband were huge at the time and I met Paddy in London. It was cheeky of me to ask them to play it, but it was no problem. Paddy wrote out the dots and they got up on the stage and played it, with me singing. The crowd loved it and it was great to have the Capitol playing it with me. The song became a hit and Paddy and the Capitol had an input in getting it there.'

Gay Byrne is more sympathetic to Cole's singing.

'Yes, of course, he can sing,' he says. 'What singing are you talking about? John McCormack, he ain't. Pavorotti, he ain't, but he can belt out a song and it's perfectly in keeping with the sort of music he makes. Most of my experience of Paddy comes from the sessions in Donegal with Paul Sweeney, Eamonn Monahan and maybe Jimmy McKay and Jack Daly. He's great fun, is a terrific story teller and great company. I don't think I've ever seen him in bad humour in all the years I've known him. A great fellow to be with for a night out, or even a day. He is also very fit.'

Gay knows about Cole's fitness through their annual walk each summer in Donegal. Each August a regular group, known as the Blue Stack Ramblers, set aside a day for a long walk in Donegal.

The group consists of Gay Byrne and his wife, Kathleen Watkins, Paul and Catherine Sweeney, Paddy and Helen Cole, Pat and Jo Dunleavy, Páid and Bernie Sweeney, Dr Declan Bonner and his wife, Bridin, Eamonn Monahan, Mick and Ann Sherry, Justice Liam McMenamin, Marie Louise O'Donnell and Mairead Bushnell.

After a 15 mile walk or more, the group retires to Iggie Murray's pub in Kincasslagh for a music session which continues until the early hours in one of the local houses. There is also a regular holiday in Tenerife with a group of friends each January after the busy Christmas period.

For the past 14 years Paddy and Helen have travelled to the sun with Evan and Nuala Henry, Joe and Therese Quinn, Maeve Little, Jennifer Lavelle, Brian and Patricia Carney and the infamous Gloss who takes care of everybody. The break prepares Paddy for the coming year's demands.

Paddy Cole claims he is not ready to retire. 'I can't afford to,' he quips. 'I have put an awful lot of effort and investment into what I'm doing now.' These days, in addition to his regular gigs, he is increasingly sought by agencies for corporate functions. Some of the agents, notably Marjorie Courtney, are close friends. 'Marjorie is very efficient, and when we do gigs for her, we always know it will be very well organised. That means a lot to us.'

But it is a strain, trying to be a performer 24 hours a day. 'Often my wife, Helen, and my family would prefer I was doing less, and I do get very tired sometimes and I should listen to Helen more often. She is still my best friend.'

'Looking back, I have no regrets. I think a lot about my father, who died in 1981. When good things happen, like the TV series, I keep thinking of him.

'I like to make people happy. It gives me great satisfaction. You meet some knockers, but there are more decent people out there than the other kind.'

Nowhere did the TV series cause more excitement than in the Cole home in 'Blaney where it was avidly watched by Paddy's mother, Mary and his older sister, Sadie. As an only son, there is a special bond between Paddy and his mother. From the start she has closely monitored his career.

'When he was away on tours, Mummy would always worry about him,' his sister Mae recalls. 'When Acker Bilk would come on the radio, playing *Stranger on the Shore*, she would go very quiet and the tears would flood into her eyes as it reminded her of Paddy.'

There are still regular phone calls between mother and son, with a special one each Sunday evening at 8p.m. before Paddy heads for the Harcourt Hotel. No matter where she is, Mary Cole insists on being home by eight o'clock to take this special call. During the summer sessions in the nearby Glencarn Hotel in Castleblaney, she is a regular fan. If his mother still worries about his wellbeing, his sister Sadie's concern is about his spiritual welfare.

'Have you been down on your knees this morning, Paddy?' she regularly asks him on the days when he stays over in 'Blaney?'

'Sure, Sadie,' he jibes, 'I dropped a fiver under the bed!'

Paddy and Helen Cole with President Mary Robinson at her celebration function in the Burlington Hotel in November 1990.

Theresa Logue, widow of Terry Logue of The Clipper Carlton, presents his saxaphone to Paddy Cole in the Harcourt Hotel in September 1995.

The *Craic 'n' Cole* series brought a flood of fan mail. One letter which delighted Cole came from 13 year-old Lisa Hurley from College Road, Cork City.

She wrote:

'Dear Mr Cole

Hi! My name is Lisa and I'm 13 years old. Ever since I was a little kid, I have always loved jazz music and have always wanted a saxophone. One year Mum and Dad took me and my brother to the Opera House at the Cork Jazz weekend, and I loved every bit of it.

Now that your show is on, I always look forward to Saturday night. I love your show, and the band are brilliant, too!

I have a clarinet, too. I got it for my birthday. I've only had it a month now, but already I can play a few tunes on it. I can never get the same sound of it, though, as you can! And when my lungs get used to blowing into a clarinet, I'll be going on to a tenor saxophone.

Well, I think your show is absolutely brilliant. If it's no trouble, would you please send me your autograph. Thanks. I was really bummed out when I heard your show was in Cork and I wasn't at it. But that's what television is for!

Best wishes for the future.

Yours truly

Lisa Hurley.

'Lisa is 13!,' says Cole. 'That's old. I was playing on stage at 12!'

Gerry and Elizabeth O'Connor join Paddy Cole for a blow in the Paddy Cole Bar in the Blarney Park Hotel.